Impressions of Cuba in the Nineteenth Century

The Travel Diary of Joseph J. Dimock

Edited by Louis A. Pérez

A Scholarly Resources Inc. Imprint
Wilmington, Delaware

Scholarly Resources Inc.
104 Greenhill Avenue
Wilmington, DE 19805-1897

Library of Congress Cataloging-in-Publication Data

Dimock, Joseph Judson, 1827–1862.
  Impressions of Cuba in the nineteenth century : the travel diary of Joseph J. Dimock / edited by Louis A. Pérez.
        p.   cm. — (Latin American silhouettes : studies in history and culture)
    Includes bibliographical references and index.
    ISBN 0-8420-2657-6 (cloth : alk. paper). —
ISBN 0-8420-2658-4 (paper : alk. paper)
    1. Cuba—Description and travel. 2. Dimock, Joseph Judson, 1827–1862—Diaries. 3. Cuba—Social life and customs. 4. Dimock, Joseph Judson, 1827–1862—Journeys—Cuba. I. Pérez, Louis A., 1943–   . II. Title. III. Series: Latin American silhouettes.
F1763.D56   1998
917.29104'5—dc21   97-34086
                                                            CIP

⊗ The paper used in this publication meets the minimum requirements of the American National Standard for permanence of paper for printed library materials, Z39.48, 1984.

For Helen, a traveler of vast distances

⌇ About the Editor ⌇

Louis A. Peréz, Jr., is J. Carlyle Sitterson Professor of History at the University of North Carolina at Chapel Hill. His previous books include *Cuba between Empires, 1878–1902* (1983), *Cuba: Between Reform and Revolution*, 2d ed. (1995), and *Cuba and the United States: Ties of Singular Intimacy*, 2d ed. (1997).

ᔕ Contents ᔕ

Introduction, **ix**

February 1859, **1**

March 1859, **71**

Bibliographical Essay: Selected Travel Titles, **147**

≈ Introduction ≈

The middle decades of the nineteenth century were remarkable years in Cuba, a time of slave conspiracies and annexationist plots, of filibustering invasions from without and colonial insurrection from within, years of economic expansion, and of political intrigue. These were also the decades of manifest destiny in the United States, and indeed nothing seemed more manifestly destined than the annexation of Cuba. Many believed that the time for union was right since the success of militant expansion westward seemed to portend expansion southward.

Developments in Cuba were not unconnected to events in the United States. Annexationist stirrings peaked and subsided in both countries during the 1840s and 1850s. In the United States, expansionist elements were in the political ascendancy and pursued the acquisition of Cuba with new purposefulness. War with Mexico had resulted in a vast increase of national territory, and many North Americans seemed to want more. This was the age of filibusters. William Walker planned to seize Nicaragua, and John Quitman dreamed of Cuban annexation to maintain southern parity for slave states. In 1848, President James K. Polk offered Spain $100 million for the island, without success. At about the same time, filibuster Narciso López mounted three successive filibustering invasions of Cuba—one in 1848 to Manicaragua, another in 1849 in Cárdenas, and the last one in 1851 to Bahía Honda, where he was finally captured and subsequently executed. In early 1854 the administration of President Franklin Pierce again tendered a purchase offer to Spain for Cuba, thereby raising the bid to $130 million but with no more success than the previous offer. Some months later, U.S. ministers to Spain, France, and England met in Ostend, Belgium, and publicly urged the United States to renew its offer to purchase Cuba. The Ostend Manifesto, as the declaration became known, ended on an ominous note, warning that if Spain refused to sell the island, "then, by every law, human and divine, we shall be justified in wresting it from Spain if we possess the power."

The Cuban economy increasingly assumed definitive form around structural linkages to the United States. A wide range of new dependencies developed, almost all of which required North American markets, capital, and technology. Between 1841 and 1859 the value of Cuban imports from the United States increased from $27.8 million to $40.3 million, while the value of exports to the North grew from $37.4 million to $68.3 million. No less important, sugar exports, a growing percentage of the source of total foreign exchange, increased from 100 tons in 1840 to 477 tons in 1860, even as the portion reaching the United States rose from 42 tons (42 percent) to 296 tons (62 percent). By midcentury the defining features of the Cuban economy were assuming discernible form.

These patterns were established early and served mutual needs. Having lost access to British West Indian tropical products, the newly independent thirteen colonies of North America searched for substitute sources, even as Cuban producers sought new markets for expanding sugar production. The timing was fortuitous. The United States was an ideal trading partner because of its proximity, its dynamic merchant marine, growing population, rising demand, and expanding economy. The United States was also an important source of Cuban imports, since it was a market for Cuban exports. It was this factor that figured prominently into the commercial strategies of merchants from both countries.

North American traders shrewdly pursued the Cuban market, providing slaves and manufactured goods at reasonable prices, often extending generous credit arrangements and accepting sugar and molasses as payment. The market was to have far-reaching implications. That Cubans could expand production for export at the expense of production for consumption as both a profitable and practical strategy was due principally to their ability to remedy local shortages with foreign supplies. Indeed, it was more cost effective to rely on food imports for the local market than sacrifice sugar exports to foreign markets. That the United States could meet these needs, as well as provide Cuba with vital industrial supplies, for comparatively short distances in a relatively short period of time and at low transportation costs, encouraged and facilitated the expansion of Cuban sugar production.

Contacts expanded rapidly. The number of North American ships arriving at Cuban ports increased from 150 in 1796, to 606 in 1800, 783 in 1826, 1,702 in 1846, and 1,886 in 1852. Commerce flourished and trade volume increased steadily. North American ships originating from Boston, New York, Philadelphia, Savannah, and New Orleans provided Cubans with box shoots, staves, caskets, barrels, hoops, nails, tar, textiles, salt, fish, corn, lard, flour, and rice. They returned to the United States loaded with sugar, tobacco, molasses, and coffee.

The inexorable logic of circumstances transformed the United States into Cuba's single most important trading partner. Together, the United States, England, and Spain accounted for almost 80 percent of the island's total foreign trade. In 1850, Cuban trade with the United States represented 39 percent of this total, followed by England (34 percent) and Spain (27 percent). Nine years later the U.S. share rose to 48 percent. In the following decades, Cuban trade patterns were even more striking. By 1865 the island exported 65 percent of its sugar to the United States and 3 percent to Spain.

The importance of Spanish participation in the Cuban economy was diminishing. Spain could neither offer Cuban producers adequate markets nor guarantee Cuban consumers sufficient supplies. The United States offered both. Spain had lost the capacity to consume all of Cuba's sugar exports and without refinery capability lacked the means to reexport Cuban sugar to other markets. At the same time, North American capital in Cuba increased in value and variety. Although comparatively few in number, North Americans were actively involved in strategic sectors of the economy, expanding into transportation and communications, purchasing sugar mills and coffee farms, and buying ranches and mines. Increasingly, they bought plantations, thereby adding further to the potency of the North American presence. As early as 1823 an estimated fifty North Americans owned plantations valued at more than three million dollars in Matanzas alone. As early as 1833, U.S. investors acquired interests in the Juraguá iron mines near Santiago de Cuba. Other U.S. claims followed in quick succession: copper mines in El Cobre, iron mines in Daiquirí and Manicaragua, and the Bayestabo mines in Nuevitas (American Mining Company). Thomas B. Smith and Heze-kiah Bradford operated the Compañía de Minería Cubana near Cienfuegos. The New York Ore Dressing Company owed mines in El Cobre.

North American merchant houses soon became a ubiquitous presence across the island, expanding along both coasts and into almost every province, most notably in Havana, Matanzas, Cienfuegos, Cárdenas, Sagua la Grande, Trinidad, and Santiago de Cuba. They summoned into existence alternative financial structures, new insurance systems, and additional shipping agencies, thereby creating ties that were at once reciprocal and structural. Furthermore, merchant houses provided credit and supplies, facilitated the movement of cargo, and aided in the distribution of imports, all of which further implicated North Americans in Cuba's economic development. At least as important, they controlled the service linking Cuban trade with New Orleans, Savannah, Charleston, Baltimore, Philadelphia, New York, and Boston.

The establishment of these connections further stimulated the value and volume of the Cuba-U.S. trade. More and more, too, U.S. capital goods became vital factors in the expansion of industrial and transportation infrastructure of the island. Steam-coast shipping, railroads, steam-powered engines, and telegraph lines were only some of the most prominent developments introduced by North American investors, whose presence presaged the new order of things. Their influence knew no boundaries and simultaneously expanded into many directions. Cubans, in turn, were becoming increasingly dependent on the United States for technology and technicians as well as for its markets, imports, capital, and credit. Above all, this relationship served to foster and facilitate the integration of the Cuban economy into the North American system. This presence and the growing importance of the North American connection worked powerfully to weaken Cuban political, economic, and cultural connections to Spain.

In the process a flourishing North American community developed in Cuba. Its principal population center—approximately twenty-five hundred—was located in Havana, where mostly merchants, importers, planters, merchants, and retailers lived. Similar, if smaller, U.S. communities formed in Matanzas, Cienfuegos, Cárdenas, and Santiago de Cuba, and many of their residents married into prominent creole families. Others arrived to operate the expanding Cuban industrial manufactures imported from the United States, especially the modern steam-powered mill machinery and railroad locomotives, and to work on the tracks and rail lines. North American *maquinistas* (machinists) arrived in the fall and remained through June for the duration of the sugar harvest to service the vast industrial complex around which the Cuban sugar industry had organized. North Americans operated hotels and restaurants, catering to and thereby fostering the expansion of the tourist trade, which was made up mostly of North Americans. Such establishments as the Washington Hotel, the American Hotel, the Ensor House, and the Hewitt House developed as centers of U.S. vacation travel to the island. An estimated five thousand North American tourists visited the island annually, mostly to escape the rigors of the winters of the northern latitudes.

Travel was indeed popular at midcentury. As the select bibliography of published travel accounts included in this volume suggests, the mid-decades of the nineteenth century were a time of extensive travel interest in Cuba. Talk of annexation brought Cuba to the attention of the larger public in the United States. Certainly, too, growing North American business interests could only have increased travel to Cuba. Improved transportation encouraged journeys to the island, and the inauguration of scheduled steamship service between Cuba and points north, principally to New Orleans, New York, and New England, played an important part in the expansion of travel. The declining commercial maritime activity between Cuba and Spain also reduced the only means of passage be-

tween the island and the Iberian Peninsula. As passenger travel between Cuba and the United States
expanded and improved, transatlantic maritime service between Cuba and Spain became increasingly
irregular, infrequent, and unreliable. As the number of
vessels in service declined, the quality of passenger
travel deteriorated. At the same time, U.S. merchant
fleets expanded, service improved, and steamships re-
placed sailing vessels, thereby reducing travel time. A
voyage to New York was completed in less than four
days and to New Orleans in half that time. Passage to
Spain often required only two weeks, but given the
infrequency of shipping and the unreliability of service,
the trip often took two and three times that long. These
developments had far-reaching implications and
served to reinforce influences already in the making.

    Not much is known about Joseph J. Dimock. He
was born in Petersburg, Virginia, in 1827 and was subsequently educated in Connecticut. Upon completing
his schooling, he worked as a mercantile agent in Boston, New York, and New Haven. He married Isadora
DeWolf in 1857, and it was through his wife's family
that Dimock established his connection to Cuba.
George DeWolf operated a sugar estate near
Cienfuegos along the south coast, and James DeWolf
owned the San Juan Mill in Matanzas on the north
coast. Dimock's trip to Cuba, at the request of the
DeWolf family, involved business transactions on the
island. During the Civil War, he subsequently served
as major in the 82nd Regiment of the New York Volunteers. He died of typhoid fever during the Peninsular
Campaign of 1862.

    Dimock's diary spans February and March 1859.
His itinerary on the island took him from Havana to
Regla, Matanzas, Cárdenas, and Recreo and then all
along the north coast of the provinces of Havana and
Matanzas. The original manuscript copy of the diary,

located in the Special Collections Department of the Robert W. Woodruff Library at Emory University, is in remarkably well-preserved condition. Only in a few places did defects in the original manuscript make a portion of an entry illegible, and, in such places, ellipses have been used to indicate unreadable text. Dimock's underlining of words and phrases has been maintained; however, inconsistencies in spelling and capitalization have been corrected. Since Dimock frequently placed information within parentheses, for clarity the editor has used brackets to indicate that a letter or word has been inserted.

Finally, there is the curious anomaly of Dimock's incorporation of previously published material into his diary. As was customary at the time, Dimock undoubtedly traveled to Cuba equipped with the most recently published guidebook to the island, both as a source of information and as a means of orientation. In this instance, it was the well-written and informative account completed by Maturin M. Ballou, *History of Cuba; or Notes of a Traveller in the Tropics*, published in Boston in 1854. At several points there are passages in the Dimock diary copied directly from or based on Ballou's *History of Cuba*.

The publication of Dimock's diary was made possible as a result of the cooperation and collaboration of many people. First and foremost, I would like to express my heartfelt appreciation to Mr. and Mrs. Joseph J. Dimock IV for their assistance all through the time in which the diary was being prepared for publication. They were enormously helpful, providing assistance at every step of the way, including the furnishing of biographical information and the photograph that accompanies this volume. I also would like to thank the staff at the Special Collections Department at the Robert W. Woodruff Library at Emory University for graciously providing permission for publication. Carole L. Rennick converted the original handwritten diary into typescript, and hence completed that all-important phase without which nothing else would have been possible, and for which I am deeply grateful. I owe also an enormous appreciation to Rosalie Radcliffe for her assistance in the final preparation of the manuscript. Finally, I would like to acknowledge the support and patience—and especially the latter—of Richard Hopper of Scholarly Resources all the long while that this manuscript was overdue. He is an ideal author's editor.

L. A. P., Jr.
Chapel Hill, NC

Tuesday, February 2, 1859

A PLEASANT MORNING but toward noon the weather becomes uncomfortable and blustering. On board steamer, *Empire City*, at twelve o'clk with Cousin Anita. Several friends come down to see us off, but I was in "a state of mind" in consequence of not getting my trunk and carpet bag in which I had laid in a store of conveniences for the voyage such as books, cigars, seidlitz powders etc. The stupid porter at the Metropolitan (though repeatedly directed) took my baggage on board a steamer for Savannah, instead of Havana. All the baggage with me consisted of a bottle of good brandy which Warren Leland placed in my hands on leaving the hotel. At two o'clk promptly the steamer left the wharf and I started for the tropics without a change of linen. Having a lady with me and expecting my luggage every moment until we started I could not give up the voyage. We left the wharf with the farewells and cheers of our friends and a parting gun from the quarterdeck of the steamship *Illinois* which lay the other side of our pier. As we sailed down the bay the weather became thick astern and we could see a snow storm following close in our wake but we had out-stripped it before getting to Sandy Hook. By this time my companion and most of the female passengers had retired to their berths <u>getting ready to be seasick</u>. I find the Purser Mr. Denison a fine

1

sociable fellow and he has kindly offered me the use of any portion of his wardrobe during the passage. Also a fellow passenger Mr. Willard Everett of Boston has made me the same offer, so I presume by the aid of these friends and a pocket comb, I shall get comfortably to Havana. Went down to the supper table at six bells, and felt better after eating and a cup of tea. Afterward Mr. Everett and myself tried the flavor of my bottle of brandy as a preventative for seasickness and after a few games of "old sledge" turned in about nine o'clk. The sea was getting somewhat rough and I found the berth the most comfortable place. Thought how friends at home must be thinking of one out on the sea, away from those he loves best.

Thursday, February 3

STORMY AND ROUGH and not having on my sea legs, kept to my berth a great portion of the day. Our cabin stove would not draw and the cabin was cold and uncomfortable. Thermometer about 40° some 10° improvement on yesterday. Read a little, but slept more, and eat and drank but little. Not seasick but no confidence in legs or stomach.

Friday, February 4

FINE DAY but head winds and sea rough. Crossed other side of gulf stream this afternoon, off

Cape Hatteras this noon. Not warm yet, but a gradual rise of the thermometer. Not seasick, but no great appetite. Passengers scarce at the table.

Saturday, February 5

CLEAR DAY and not as rough, good appetite and on deck most of the day. Obliged Anita to come out on deck and take some fresh air. The passengers begin to crawl out from their state rooms and take their seats at the table. At noon Lat 32-18 about 150 miles from Cape Fear below Charleston. Air warmer and thermometer 66° at noon. Doctor pronounces me very billious and prescribes [. . .] Hydrarg and Ext Colocynth Comp. and seidlitz powders every morning following.

Sunday, February 6

A BEAUTIFUL DAY, and smooth sea, steamer runs as easy as on a river, Lat 29-23. All passengers on deck today and table well filled at dinner. Captain Griffin very pleasant gentleman and very agreeable. Spend a great portion of the time in his office and with the purser in his room. Clear and moonlight evening and thermometer at 74°. About seven o'clk P.M. one of our steerage passengers named <u>Claude Rodrot</u> jumped overboard from quarterdeck and was lost. Steamer put about, but could find no trace of him.

Monday, February 7

CLOUDY AND RAINY—showers all day but sun warm, thermometer about 76°. Saw land this afternoon and two lighthouses—off the Bahama Banks. Passed Isaac's and Gun Cays and several others. Played chess, read, wrote, and passed a very comfortable day.

Tuesday, February 8

CLEAR AND WARM, thermometer 78° at noon. Coast of Cuba in sight this afternoon. Cardenas Light and then the Pan of Matanzas. All the passengers elated at the prospect of going into Havana tomorrow morning. All up on deck till a late hour. Saw Moro light before turning in.

Wednesday, February 9

OFF THE ENTRANCE to harbor of Havana at four o'clk, and going in at sunrise. Warm day and thermometer at 84°. Customhouse officers on board, and after inspection, allowed us to go ashore. Arrived at Madame Almy's Hotel d'Luz at eight o'clk. Met the Misses Fales, and Ed Wilson. Mr. Fales met us at the customhouse. After breakfast, Wilson and self went on a shopping expedition, and the result of two hours labor was two pair of pantalones, two camisas, two pair calzones, a chaleco, a vestido, colleras and a sombrero. After which, feeling more comfortable, went into the Cafe Dominica, and indulged in a smile and smoke. Met here Captain Griffin and the medico from the *Empire City* and other friends. We dined at three o'clk and at the hotel met friend, Doringh, just came down from the country. He was somewhat surprised to find us here but pleased nevertheless. In the evening walked up to the Plaza d'Armas, to hear the band play. Bought a few cigars at cabarjos and looked about the city. Mr. Doringh has had our passport vised, and took out a landing permit, and a domicilio, giving us leaves to reside two months on the island etc. Busy day and pretty tired. Wilson and myself are fortunate to secure a good room at Mrs. Almy's.

Thursday, February 10

To A STRANGER everything looks strange in Havana. The first thing that attracted my attention was the unwieldy vehicle called the volante. It is built somewhat like our old-fashioned chaise with the body fastened to the thills or bars, and a pair of enormous wheels some few feet behind the body. The driver is mounted on the horse that draws the volante or one by its side and leading the horse in the bars, and propels the entire machine by the aid of whip and spurs. Some of these volantes are very expensively got up, with silver ornaments, velvet linings etc., and the calesero, or driver, rigged up equal to the monkey who rides in the menagerie. You will see him with a scarlet jacket covered with gold and silver lace, a sombrero, of extensive dimensions, covered with cord and brickle and a pair of tremendous jack boots reaching up in the waist, and terminating at the heel with a spur of great horse power. The streets here are very narrow, only averaging some sixteen or twenty feet in width and are badly paved while the sidewalks, where there are any, are about eighteen inches wide, and one can hardly keep on them; in passing one individual must step into the street. The houses are curiosities, being built after the old Moorish style—walls several feet in thickness, windows all iron barred, as our prisons, and no glass. They have inside shutters of wood and iron, which can be closed in very bad weather. The roofs and floors are tiled, and I have not seen a carpet in Havana. In bedrooms, a rug or mat is laid in front of the bed and a curtain before the window, but in passing in the streets one can look through the bars of the windows and observe the family at their various occupations. Some of the wealthiest and most aristocratic families live in dirty narrow streets, and while one house may be a palace, the next may be a hovel filled with the lowest of negroes. Some of the finest houses, even that of the Captain General, have stores and shops on the lower floor. Most of the families of any means keep a volante, for the ladies never walk in the streets; and the main or principal entrance to the house is a large door through which driver and carriage enter into a kind of courtyard which is surrounded by the house which can be entered by ascending the stairs from the inside in case they are more than one story in height. Many houses have overhanging balconies and sometimes they project so far on each side as almost to obstruct the light from above. The houses are of every variety of color, bright blue, yellow, green, etc. Went to the theatre Villanueva this evening to hear the opera (Gazzaniga and troupe). Maretzek gave some offence to the Captain General who between the second and third act ordered the theatre closed immediately, so with others, Wilson, and self were compelled to "vamose the ranch." Concha was guarded in and guarded out of the theatre and had a file of soldiers at the door of his box. He was accompanied by his two daughters (very good looking girls), and a clownish looking aid d'camp who appeared to be about sixteen years of age, and from his orders and decorations was undoubtedly a count or marquis at the very least. Directly opposite the royal box was seated one of his numerous mistresses (lately cast off) who, from the significant look she occasionally gave, seemed to be in anything but good humor. By her side was the wife of Santa Anna, of Mexican fame, apparently a clever but dull looking woman, of dark complexion and rather robust. The beauty of Havana were all present, such as they are. The beauty of the Spanish women consists of their magnificent proportions and a fine head of hair; but of the hundreds of ladies present, I saw but two or three of delicate figures. I should judge the average weight of the ladies to be about 160 lbs, the only real handsome girls in the theatre were our Yankee girls. Nellie and Caro Fales with Madame F. in her box and the Spaniards seemed to think so for they stared without cessation at what they termed "lindas Americanas" (beautiful Americans).

Friday, February 11

SINCE OUR ARRIVAL here, the thermometer has been as high as 85° but the average heat at this season is about 75°. It looks odd enough to me on the eleventh of February to be dressed in linen coat and pants, sleeping with windows and doors open in the bedroom, and finding on the table, green peas, plantains, beans, lettuce, yams, tomatoes, etc., and for dessert to eat oranges, bananas and coconuts, fresh from the trees. I may be better able to give a more correct and ample idea Cuban dishes and table, but suffice it to say that here of good things eatable and drinkable there is no end. Went out with Wilson this afternoon to the <u>Campo Marte</u> or Field of Mars, to see a drill of some of the Spanish soldiers. This field is a fine level piece of ground of some ten acres. I should judge devoted to military purposes, for drill, etc. My impressions of the Spanish military force, their drill discipline, etc., are anything but favorable. So far they have excited my visibility to a great extent. Compared with our volunteer militia, they are <u>below par,</u> and the scholars of the military schools at New Haven excel them in everything that should make a good soldier. They are said to be capable of great endurance, which I think must be true, as they are enabled to endure so much filth etc., on their uniforms and faces. We saw a battalion of the <u>regulars</u> go through the light infantry drills (a la Hardee in the States); the style in which they performed was inimitable and would provoke a laugh from the veriest [. . .] in military affairs. In skirmishing the soldiers walked leisurely up and down the parade; and in retreating and forming line, each faced about and took his position as accorded with his own individual convenience. They carried a kind of musketoon, with sword-bayonet, from the careless manner of swinging them about, each soldier was in danger from his neighbor. It is no wonder that in actual service so many of the Spanish soldiers are shot in the back. This reminds me of the Spanish general, Ena, who was killed at the battle of San Rosas while attacking Lopez. He was shot in the back of the head! A splendid monument was erected to his memory by the engineers of his brave army, and stands in the centre of the <u>Paseo d'Isabel Sequnda</u>. It is surmounted by a colosal statue of Queen Isabella in coronation robes and as a work of art is really beautiful. There is also a fine statue (also of white marble) of Carlos III in the centre of the Plaza d'Armas fronting the palace or house of the Captain General and one also of King Ferdinand on the <u>paseo</u> running to Fort Principe. On the Alameda d'Paula just below our hotel and fronting the quays stand the remains of a fine piece of sculpture. It is a pillar of white marble, richly embossed and was surmounted by the Spanish lion crowned. Below was a fine basin, and water gushed out from the four sides of the pedestal through the mouths of four more Spanish lions. Just about the time of Lopez's second landing on the island, this column was struck by lightning and completely dismantled and disfigured. It stands now just as the lightning left it, the water dried up, and the lions broken to fragments and lying in the basin. The Spaniards are naturally very superstitious and at the time considered this a fearful omen of evil things to come, and have not as yet had courage or spirit enough (though nearly eight years have passed) to repair it. There was a grand serenade at the plaza tonight given to the Captain General by the volunteers of Havana, in honor of his expected departure for the Peninsula. All the crack band of the army, the opera troupe etc., joined in vocal and instrumental music. The sight was a brilliant one and we who took ladies with us enjoyed it, for we had the "lindas Americanas." The soldiers' vivas, and "long live Isabel and Spain," etc., were coldly received by the masses, and the soldiers only cheered while the spectators quietly laughed at the demonstration. It was intended for a great ovation to Concha previous to his departure but for a political demonstration it was a complete failure. The Captain General was so much cut up by it that he refused to show himself on the balcony to his "ever faithful" subjects as is customary. Concha never goes about the city without his mounted guard of a hundred lancers, and it is evident from the precautions taken by him that he does not consider himself safe without them. The Cubans (criollos) say if found alone in the streets he would be assassinated.

The Plaza d'Armas is an open square in front of the Captain General's residence, in the centre of which stands the statue of Carlos III and surrounded by a beautiful flower garden and a few palm trees. Directly opposite stands a little chapel, said to be the identical and sacred spot where Columbus landed, and where Mass was first said. The large ceiba tree under which Columbus and his followers knelt still stands, at least tradition says it is the same tree, and the Spaniards look upon it with a veneration similar to that which our Connecticut people had for our own Charter Oak. On the opposite side of the square, stands the residence of the Captain General, a long oriental building supported in front by arches, two stories in height, and apparently very substantial. On another side of the square stands the treasury buildings and barracks, and in this vicinity the soldiers are so thick that it is difficult to pass without treading on them. This is <u>almost</u> literally true, for the soldiers are nearly all very small undersized men, and have the general air and appearance (in their nondescript uniform) of state prison convicts.

The old cathedral nearby is a venerable pile, built after the old Moorish style, and of great strength and durability. Here repose the ashes of the great discoverer Christopher Columbus, who was everything to Spain, but fortunately for his memory was indebted to another country for his birth.

It is computed that there are in Havana for every ten white men, one soldier, as there are stationed here of the regular army alone over ten thousand troops, this not including municipal police, <u>voluntarios</u> or volunteers of Havana (a militia organization), watchmen, etc., who are all armed and uniformed. This also does not include a battalion of negroes who honorably support the arms and uniform of her Majesty the Queen.

The laboring people of Havana, (draymen, porters, etc.) are generally of the very lowest class, and as degraded as is possible for human beings. The negroes are most of them pictures of ugliness, frightful to behold, of the true baboon class, projecting muzzle and retreating chin and forehead. They are rarely more than half clothed and their general appearance is very repulsive. They are of inky blackness and would probably rejoice the heart of any true amalgamationist.

As one enters the harbor of Havana the view is charming. The hills about the city are covered with verdure, and the waving palm and coconut trees impress one favorably with the tropics. The immense fortifications of the Moro Castle and the Fort of Cabanas guard the entrance to the harbor, while the point of land directly opposite is defended by the Punta Fort, where is kept the <u>garrote</u> on which Lopez and other brave Creoles forfeited their lives for the sake of "beloved Cuba." In the rear of this fort is the immense, new prison building, and barracks for the soldiers, a splendid building of buff colored limestone. On the south side of the city on the summit of high hills are Forts Atares and Principe. On the sloping side of the hills under the walls of the former is where Crittenden and his young companions were massacred for daring to assist in the liberation of Cuba. We shall probably live to see the time when their names will be inscribed on lasting monuments as the first victims of Cuban independence. I have taken pains to talk with intelligent Cubans as to the general feeling here toward the Spanish government, and am surprised to hear how openly and freely they express their hatred and contempt for their rulers. There is no sympathy between the Spaniards and Cubans and it is manifested in a thousand ways.

Wilson and self went over to Regla which is a suburb of the city on the east side of the harbor and is connected with the city by several lines of ferries. It is to Havana what Brooklyn is to New York, or rather will be when the city becomes Americanized. There are some beautiful locations there, and undoubtedly much more healthy than the city proper, as it is on the windward side, easterly winds prevail here about four-fifths of the time, but unlike our easterly winds at home they ensure a warm clear day, and only when the south winds blow strong is the heat too much for those acclimated. There are facing the wharves at Regla, long rows of sugar warehouses where the sugar is deposited as it is brought down from the interior of the island, and here inspected, classed, and marked preparatory for shipment to other countries. At the ferry landing stands the new depot of the new line of railroad now being built from Havana to Matanzas. As yet only about one-fourth (fifteen miles) of the road is completed. The building is a fine one covered with stucco, and has some pretensions to architectural beauty, and arranged after the style of our railroad depots at the north. I noticed the cars and locomotives were all of American manufacture, being mostly made in

Jersey City, and that only American engineers had charge of the locomotives. The ferryboat[s] running over here are also all built in the United States. Some were named *Guanabacoa, General Concha,* [. . .] *Isabel 2nd,* etc. I saw here employed about the sugar warehouses, great numbers of Chinese coolies, mostly dressed with only a straw hat and a pair of pantaloons, or a cloth wound around their loins and hips. They are apparently but little better than idiots in point of intellect, and it is said that even the niggers feel above them. While here we patronized an old darkey and made a splendid lunch on fresh oranges, bananas and coconut milk.

Went up town as far as the plaza, called into a bank with Wilson and liked their manner of doing business, very polite cashier, teller, etc., and they pay out nothing but gold and silver. Called in at Dominica's then for dinner.

Saturday, February 12

VISITED THE CELEBRATED fish market this morning and was amply repaid for the time. The market is a monopoly granted by one of the former Captain Generals (O'Donnell, I think) to one Martí a reformed pirate, wholly betraying his comrades into the power of the government, received the privilege of selling all the fish in Havana as a reward for his treachery. It is situated on the ramparts directly opposite the Cabanas Fortress, and is a building of about the size of our City Hall Market, but only one story in height. The water of the harbor flows underneath, and the fish are kept fresh in cars, only a few being exposed for sale at one time. I saw but few fish that I could recognize by size, shape, or color. The lobsters are of every color, and with a different kind of animal from what we see at home. The eels are from two to six feet in length and look like sea serpents, but the flavor is exquisite. The fish is the finest I ever tasted and the color alone would tempt an epicure. There were fish of every imaginable size and shape and as to color, they would almost rival the rainbow, there were hues of gold, silver, blue, green, red, yellow, and some of all colors together. The turtles too were a novelty to a Yankee, some of them weighing over five hundred pounds. Turtle soup out here is the genuine article and "no mock." I have before mentioned the Cabanas Fortress. It is a long line of fortifications built of stone and part cut out of solid rock. It comes with the Moro Castle by subterranean passage and in the dungeons underneath are confined prisoners who are supposed to have conspired against the peace and quietness of the "ever faithful island." These huge forts were finished during the reign of Charles III and originally cost millions of dollars, the cost I have heard named being almost fabulous. When it was announced to his Majesty that the Moro was finished, he ascended to the highest point of his palace in Madrid with telescope in hand to look at the famous castle in Cuba. Being told by one of his ministers that the distance was too great for it to be seen, he exclaimed, "It has cost enough to reach the heavens and to be seen all over the world." The splendid lighthouse on the outer wall of the Moro and also the telegraph station were erected by O'Donnell in 1844. The Cabanas is said to command the Moro and was once stormed by the English and through it they retained possession of the city for two years. During that time one of the churches was used by the soldiers for Protestant worship, and this fact has so defiled it in the eyes of the <u>pious</u> Spaniards, that it has never been used for devotional purposes since. Public Protestant worship is not allowed on the island, but is occasionally held on foreign vessels in the harbors, etc. I have looked into several of the churches and find them open at all times, and the lazy <u>padres</u> loafing about, the very picture of obesity. I noticed that nearly all of the attendants at the churches were of the poorer class, though occasionally a gaily dressed <u>señorita</u> would come in attended by her slave, who after brushing away the dust, would place a cushion for her to kneel upon, while by her side might kneel the filthiest of negroes, all going through the same pantomime, and all apparently sincere. There are no seats in the churches except for the priests, and here at least all are brought to the same level, all kneeling. It is said the power of the priests is passing away and I think but little respect is shown for them though the <u>power</u> of the church is as great as ever for its revenues are immense.

The stores here are very small and make but little pretention to style or size. Each <u>store</u> has a <u>name</u>. Not the name of the proprietor for that does not appear, but the <u>store</u> is named according to the fancy of the proprietor without any regard to its adaptation to the business within. For instance

I have seen "The Angel," "The Flower of Havana," "The Strong Arm," "The Little Rooster," "My Destiny," "The Green Crop," " The First Book of Paris," "The Bomb," "The Bon Ton," "The True Cross," "The Never Die," "The Goats Feet," and many other designations quite as ridiculous. I had considerable shopping to do on account of the detention of my baggage in New York and but for Ed Wilson's assistance who speaks Spanish as fluently as a native, I should have been shaved quite as close by the Spanish store keepers as ever Yankees shave. I have learned the Spanish method of counting money and by substituting <u>pesos</u> for dollars, <u>rials</u> for shilling, and <u>dinero</u> for money and <u>quanto</u> for "how much" but little difficulty is experienced. American silver will hardly pass but at a discount except dimes. Quarters are worth here but twenty cents, halves, forty cents, etc. I have not as yet seen any paper money here, all ordinary dealings are in gold and silver. Although one or two of the banks do issue bills as small as $50 but none less. In coming out here one would do well to provide himself with old Spanish quarters, ninepences and sixpences, for they pass for their full original value here. The coins in most common use are gold ounces, value $17, and half, quarter and eighth ounces in the same proportion.

The quays or wharves of Havana are very superior, beginning at the lower end of the Alameda d'Paula, and all along as far as nearly to the fish market are fine wharves, and mostly covered by a light roof supported by slender columns and built of iron. This is for the protection of merchandise and also of the laborers who are not thereby exposed to the rays of the sun, which are intolerable in the warm season. All vessels lie at the wharf stern to shore and it is a long job to discharge a large cargo by sliding down on planks from the bows to the wharf. All vessels entering must come to anchor in the harbor, which is perfectly safe and commodious, and go through a long series of formalities before they can take their turn for wharfage. The harbor is completely filled with vessels at anchor, and I notice the great proportion of them are American, a great many from "away down East" in Maine. It is estimated that two-thirds of all the shipping entering the port is American. Our trade with the island is immense, and although Cuba is a great market for American goods, yet the difference in favor of Cuba last year was over five million dollars. The enormous tax in the way of duties prevents the importation of many American goods. Our American steamers, with the exception of the *Isabel* running to Charleston, are obliged to anchor at some considerable distance from the city proper, and passengers go to and from the ship in small boats, and in bad weather it is somewhat unpleasant if not a hazardous experiment. The owners of the *Isabel*, being the first American mail steamer ever run here, shrewdly named her in honor of the Queen of Spain, and her majesty's government being flattered (as Spaniards are very easily) granted them the privilege of anchoring their steamer close to the city, which no other one can do except a Spanish vessel.

Though the Spanish nation have an open hatred of everything American, yet lately, for some reason, (perhaps the thirty million proposition) they seem to treat us with unusual respect. Americans can and do talk here openly of buying Cuba, of annexation and of <u>manifest destiny</u> and are only answered by a shrug of incredulous shoulders. Within a few days for the first time in history, our American mail steamers have been saluted by a gun from the flagship of the Spanish Admiral. What this unusual politeness portends I cannot say. A creole gentleman (Señor E.) tells me they begin to believe in manifest destiny. Certain it is, that the idea of annexation to the States is getting to be very popular here, not only among the Creoles, but among <u>young</u> Spaniards who have had an opportunity to become acquainted with American ways and means. Cuba is a garden of the world, and essential to the growth and prosperity of our union and must eventually be with us and of us.

One of the most unpleasant sights in Havana is the chain gang, working on the streets, paving, repairing, making sewers, cleaning, etc. There were white, black and mulatto as well as Chinamen, all chained two and two, and while at work, each with heavy chain riveted around the waist and ankle. Their drivers in the mongrel uniform of the soldiers are standing over them and any disposition to shirk is rewarded by a blow across the face or back, with a heavy cane or chord. Some brutal scenes are witnessed and so much unnecessary cruelty manifested, that one cannot but sympathize with the prisoners. Here are chained together, burglars, murderers, thieves, without regard to their grade of crime. All equally bad in the eyes of Spanish law, unless they have the pesetas, wherewith to bribe the officials. It has heretofore been a favorite mode with General Concha to punish creole gentlemen for political sins by sentencing them to the chain gang, and many a gentleman has been compelled for months to associate and work with some of the vilest and most abandoned of the human family.

I have spoken heretofore I think of Creoles, a wrong impression exists in the States as to the proper definition of the word "Creole"; many supposing it to imply negro or mixed blood. This is wrong and has been confounded with the Quadroon. By Creole is understood here, all who have been born on the island without regard to sex or color. The white Creoles are denied many privileges allowed to Spanish born, and there seems to be a natural enmity between them. No Creole is allowed to hold any official position either civil or military on the island.

The names of the streets here are comical to a stranger, Calle de O'Reilly is O'Riley Street, there is too Calle Jesus Maria, Calle Inquisidor, Calle d'Lamparilla and Calle Mercadores. I notice on many stores "English spoken here" but on entering a Yankee would be puzzled to understand the English. Over many I see "por mayor y menor," which is by wholesale and retail, none of the storekeepers have their names on the store, but for additional security and luck they frequently post the name of the trinity or some of the saints on the side or over the door. On one store in Calle del Rey Inteniente (King's Lieutenant Street) I think I saw on the doorpost, "N.B. Jesus Christo" (Our Lord Jesus Christ). Rarely ladies are seen walking in the street unless they are English or Americans, but negresses and low Spanish duennas, homely enough to frighten a man, are seen going to market or in and out of church from Mass, etc. One cannot turn without seeing soldiers everywhere and of all colors too. The uniform of a great portion seems to be an everyday dress of some blue mixed linen cloth, fatigue jacket and pants, and a large panama hat, with a little red slip of cloth by the side of the crown, with a little metal ornament to designate the arm of the service to which they are attached. The officers dress the same style but a finer material of cloth. The regiment or guard at Captain General's palace, etc., the artillery wear white linen jacket and pants with red trimmings and the ordinary leather military cap, with pompon, etc. Some of the lancers and mounted police guard wear white and buff uniforms with yellow trimmings and cocked or three corner hats, carrying long lances tipped with ribbons of red and yellow and carrying also sword and pistols. One of the most noted places in Havana is the Cafe Dominica, or coffee house of Señor Dominica. It is a large saloon something in the style of Taylors in B'way only not as large and clean, for these Spaniards are about the dirtiest people extant. In the centre of a large open courtyard covered by awnings, etc., is a beautiful fountain, with water trickling over the rocks, and the wild aquatic plants of the tropics, trailing from the ledge. Here may be seen at all hours, the Havaneros eating and drinking, for they eat sweetmeats or dulces at any time for they have a terrible sweet tooth, and it is amusing to hear them call for the different

American drinks. There are no terms or words in Spanish to express many of them so they call for "brandee punnsch," "geen cotell," etc., etc. The favorite beverages of both Spaniards and Creoles seems to be a mixture of eggs and wine, fresh grape juice, orcharda (being an emulsion of almonds and sweetened water) pinales (a lemonade) and claret in endless profusion. Claret, or a species of it, called Catalan wine, is in fact on the table at every meal and drank diluted with water, by old and young of both sexes. It can be bought from forty to fifty cents a gallon and has an agreeable but pungent flavor, but nearly as strong as brandy when drank clear. At Dominica's, ladies come and here one may see evenings some of the bright eyed señoritas but the old hags of señoras or duennas are always with them. One can also always find Americans and foreigners here for this is a general rendezvous for all the strangers staying in Havana. All languages may be heard here, but of all I think the Spaniard is the most inveterate talker. He even beats the Frenchman in pantomime, for every sentence is illustrated by some peculiar gesture. They make many words over the most trifling matter, and while a Spaniard is giving the direction to find a certain street or locality, one might travel a mile.

The barbers here are also surgeons as in old Spain (vide Don Quixote). A day or two since I saw a queer sight in a barber's shop. On the floor seated with his back to the wall, sat the patient, and sitting in his lap astride of him was the operator. To extract a tooth he first pulled and broke it off, then he cut and dug, then pulled and rested then cut, dug and pulled again, and after going through this kind of exercise for fifteen or twenty minutes, released the patient, both being pretty well covered with blood. There are several English and American dentists here, but the Spaniards generally prefer going to the barber and often use as "they pay their money, they have their choice." The barbers also, leech, cup and bleed; the physicians only prescribe. The process of being shaved here is rather different than in the States. The barber does not lather but bathes the face with water from a crockery basin fitted to the neck and after pretty thoroughly <u>soaking</u> the face scrapes off the superfluous beard.

The ladies here ride out in volantes to do their shopping, and rarely enter the store, the salesman bringing out his goods and chaffering from the pavement. Most kinds of cloth goods and ready made clothing (linen goods being excepted) average a higher price than in New York; fancy goods, perfumery and toilet articles of French manufacture are cheaper than with us, but I find from experience that a Yankee is very apt to pay an extra percentage on account of his nationality. Colt's small size revolvers retail here for $24. I presume the duties are considerable. A panama hat costs less here than at home, but ready made clothing, boots, shoes are at least 25 percent higher than with us. Yankee patent medicines go down good here and the famous <u>Zarsaparilla de Bristol</u>, which is almost out of the market North, is all the go here. And the only ink used or sold as I can see is of the famous kind manufactured by Maynard and Noyes of Boston. American hardware goods I find none of, nothing being sold here but those of clumsy Spanish or German manufacture. I haven't seen a doorknob or latch yet, the only things used for fastenings, etc., are hooks and straps, huge bars and antique locks whose keys would not go into an ordinary pocket. The introduction of the thousand little household furnishing elegancies in the shape of hardware goods, might be a profitable investment here.

Lottery tickets are offered you everywhere in the hotel, street cafe etc., and everybody buys. The Royal <u>Lotteria</u> is provided for by government and it is believed to be managed strictly fair. The highest prize is $100,000 and the lowest a <u>blank</u>. It is drawn on the twentieth of every month and pays a handsome revenue to government.

There are now in the harbor of Havana over thirty Spanish war vessels of every size and description, frigates, ships of the line, steamers, gun boats and tenders, numbering in all some four hundred guns. The steamers are fine models, and apparently equal to any vessels afloat, but their big frigates, and line of battle ships appear to be relics of a former age. Around their sterns may be seen lumbering galleries or promenades and the ships would be good models for a floating bathhouse. I could see no use except as a receptacle for sailors and soldiers, and to be peppered and shot at by fast sailing Yankee clippers. The marine officers are very young, most of them mere boys, without even a beard to make them look fierce. A Spanish gentleman asked one the other day, "What if this Spanish fleet should go and bombard New York?" I could not imagine such an absurdity and told him so. He said to Wilson who stood by, what would they do if ten thousand Spanish soldiers should land there. Captain F. of Sagua sitting by said, "if the soldiers behaved themselves they would not be troubled, but if they made any disturbance, they would be put into the station houses." Spaniard says, "Quien sabe." Crowds of sailors attached to this navy may be seen in the streets everyday, off duty. They are dressed in a plain sailor costume. Blue shirt and white pants, with a straw hat and on the band the name of the vessel to which they are attached. They are larger and more robust looking men than those serving in the army.

Our friends the Fales and Ned Wilson are to take the steamer this evening at ten o'clk, they go to shop at Matanzas and we have concluded to take same boat and continue on to Cardenas, so I must wind up my peregrinations in Havana for the present.

Sunday, February 13

B EFORE LEAVING Havana and going into the interior of the island it becomes necessary for me to procure a license or passport. This required a visit to the governor of Havana, and by paying dos pesos ($2), I received a permit which as it reads; "Enables newly arrived foreigners to transit in all directions on the island during one month from its date. The want of this passport implicates a fine of $10, and nobody, whatever be his rank or class, is exempted from obedience to the ruling government and police regulation and ordinances," etc., etc. This precious document is signed by the governor, and duly countersigned by the secretary, and stamped with the insignia of royalty, so I am safe under the protection of the Spanish crown for one month, after which time I must get a renewal.

At 10 o'clk last evening we embarked onboard the propeller *Commandataria* for Matanzas and Cardenas. The boat <u>could</u> accommodate sixty passengers, but that night she did accommodate, after a fashion about one hundred and thirty souls, besides the crew. We secured our berths early in the evening, and on going onboard, found them all occupied by Spanish <u>gentlemen</u>, we however insisted upon our rights, and finally <u>compelled</u> the captain to appear and substantiate our claim, and <u>Los Espanoles</u>, had to clear out which they did with a very bad grace, grumbling and cursing <u>Los Americanos</u> in Spanish, and our party retorting in plain English. Ned gave them as good as they sent in their own language and made a considerable fun for us, by his remarks about the Spaniards <u>remarkable hat</u>, which secured berths by laying it in. Take it altogether it was <u>a rich scene</u>. The berths were merely cane bottomed and furnished with one blanket and a pillow, but very comfortable and just the thing for this climate. As we steamed slowly out of Havana Harbor the view was delightful. The moon was rising majestically over Regla Bay, and poured its pure beams down gently over the phosphorescent water till the masts of the shipping and the buildings along the wharves seemed coated with silver. We glided along under the stern of the *Francisco d'Asis*, the flagship of the Admiral, past the steamers and revenue boat, the customhouse and guardship, and then in the shadow of the battlements of the Cabanas and Moro Castle. On getting outside the motion of the vessel was considerable and she tore and pitched through the waters like a thing of life. Most of the female passengers, and there were quite a number, were sick and our friends, Nellie and Caro, after holding out as long as possible, finally succumbed to the charms of seasickness. I acted as nurse and held their heads alternately, while their father and Cousin Ned snored away comfortably in their berths. Anita was not sick but cold and wore my thick overcoat which was certainly comfortable if not becoming. About twelve o'clk, all getting accustomed to it, I persuaded the ladies to go into their own cabin, but their stay was of short duration, for there all were sick and the smell was overpowering. They came out on deck and we procured blankets and pillows for them and made them comfortable till we arrived at Matanzas about three o'clk. Here a great portion of the passengers leaving and the boat being anchored they took vacant berths in our cabin and made themselves comfortable until seven o'clk in the morning, when Mr. F. and his daughters went ashore to shop in Matanzas. While our boat lay off Matanzas I had but little opportunity to see or learn anything of the city as we lie off in the harbor and the passengers are landed in small boats. I was informed that Matanzas is a city of about 25,000 inhabitants and of a more modern style than Havana. It is situated at the mouths of two rivers, the Yumuri and San Juan. I saw no wharves of any consequence and find all large vessels are unloaded by lighters. There is a plaza in front of the government house which can be seen from the harbor and is similar to the one in Havana. As we come up the harbor and glance up the beautiful hills which surround it, I began to get an idea of the Cuban country scenery. Large fields of the light green sugarcane which can be easily distinguished on account of its color, the tall palm trees towering high over all others and having a marked character which is easy to be known as a tree of tropical growth, the waving coconut and the trim looking orange trees with dark green leaves and golden fruit, the patches of plantain and banana, all pointed out to me, and almost near enough to be touched, begin to make me realize, I am in this enchanted land, this "La siempre fidelissima Isla d'Cuba."

Just before eight o'clk we steamed up and followed the shore down to Cardenas where we arrived about twelve o'clk. We landed at the lower end of the long wharf, full a mile long and there met John Henry and Vincente waiting to receive us. After congratulations etc., we walked up to Mrs. Powers' hotel where we rested, talked and lunched. John and I strolled about this place for an hour or two, and at three o'clk we are to take the cars for Recreo and from there we ride up to San Ricardo (Mr. Smith's estate). Our steamer was dirty enough though almost new being brought out from Philadelphia last November. There was one clean place on board and that was the engine room. The engineer is a genuine go-ahead shrewd

Yankee named Hibbard Sabin and was born and raised in Franklin, Connecticut. He informs me that nearly all the engineers employed on and about the island are either American or English with occasionally a Frenchman. He says he has yet to see a Spaniard competent to take charge of a steam engine. We stopped at the store of Safford and Co. on the corner of Calle Real and it was here that Lopez and his men sustained a charge of a squadron of Spanish lancers in the open street. The filibusters opened to the right and left and received them with a cross fire and not one lancer ever rode away. But Lopez had calculated on the cooperation of the creole population, and had based his calculations on the letter and promises from them, but he was disappointed, for instead of joining his little army they remained inactive or fled to the interior, dreading the vengeance of the Spaniards if Lopez failed. He remained only a day and finding a large force coming against him by sea from Matanzas, he embarked on his steamer (*Pampero*) for Key West, leaving behind him two or three men who had accidently become separated from his party. These were seized by the Spanish authorities and immediately shot. One of them was a little drummer boy about fifteen years of age, who enlisted as a drummer without knowing his destination. He begged to be allowed to write a message to his mother, but this was denied him, he was butchered and his body thrown into the sea, food for sharks. Cardenas is not very pleasantly situated, being on low swampy ground, and water can be found by digging a few inches in any of the streets during high tide. There is much stagnant water about the place, and the effluorim rising from it is anything but grateful to the olfactories. The streets are much wider than Havana, but the style of buildings very similar and not very inviting. The main street (Calle Real) is a fine broad street running through the city over a mile in length, and just outside the city proper on rising ground are some very fine private residences. The harbor is a most excellent one, broad and deep and a very extensive shipping business is done here in sugar and molasses. There are some fine wharves, one nearly a mile long. There is a large old-style cathedral in the centre of the city, and in front of it is a plaza handsomely laid out, paved, etc., after the style of the Plaza d'Armas in Havana. It will cost when finished over $40,000. A large market house was lately finished, built of white marble with a spacious dome, iron fence, etc., and would be an ornament to any of our northern cities. A handsome public hospital is also being erected on the site of the old cemetery. I visited the grounds on the hope of finding some trace of the grave of my father-in-law George D. Wolfe, but the place was nearly covered by the hospital building and the remaining portion was strewn with portions of human bones. On the old limestone wall were scratched the names of several Americans who were buried here. I could not even get any idea of the location of his grave. The form of burying the dead on this island is really revolting. Quicklime is thrown into the grave and probably the remains of but very few remain for three months without being disturbed, for the grounds are small and dug over and over again. There is no excuse for this for there is an immense extent of wasteland all over the island, it has been estimated that only about one-tenth of the island is improved, though more than four-fifths is susceptible of cultivation.

Cardenas contains about five thousand inhabitants and quite a number of these are Americans. Large quantities of sugar and molasses are annually shipped here and the place of business is rapidly increasing. Among the American merchants here I notice the firms of Safford and Co., J. M. Churchill and Co. formerly of Portland, Maine, and George Harris, formerly of Hartford. I notice among the clerks and correspondents a great many Yankees. Within a year a great number of Americans have come out here with the intention of locating. American goods are getting more common, the heavy duties make them well up in price, yet they are good time. Sugar is now very high and business good. Cardenas Harbor is full of vessels of which more than one-half are Americans, and one sees so many Yankees in the streets that it seems quite homelike here. We started for San Ricardo at three o'clk P.M. by railroad. We stopped at Mrs. Powers' hotel while in Cardenas, and here left Ned Wilson and Lavelletts while we go into the country.

Monday, February 14

WE TOOK the Jucaro (pronounced <u>Hookary</u>) railroad from Cardenas for about twenty miles, passing through a low flat country apparently within a few miles of the coast. Here I begin to form some idea of the country. We pass large fields of sugarcane with the negroes at work cutting it and occasionally, see the tall chimneys of the sugarhouses whitewashed, and the red-tiled roofs of the buildings. We see along the road patches of plantain and banana trees and everywhere around the towering palm, the <u>royal palm</u>, with its beautiful crowning head of waving green. I notice the cars and locomotives are all of American manufacture and the engineers are Yankees, but for firemen, brakemen, I see Chinese coolies. The conductor is a Spaniard, and sells the tickets at the depot giving each passenger a printed ticket which he signs after some conversation, baggage must be paid for same as passengers and ticketed also, and there seems to be no haste about it. Everything goes on leisurely and we reached our railroad termination at <u>Recreo</u> (some twenty miles) about two hours after leaving Cardenas. The cars are fitted up with cane-bottomed seats, but are very dirty and <u>everybody</u> smokes in the cars. We found Domingo (a house servant) waiting for us with horses and Antonio D'Wolf (calesero, or driver) with a volante for Anita. We rode some two or three miles to the estate <u>St. Catalina</u> owned by the Coffigny's and the administrator living on the place was a French Creole named Bittun. He could not speak a word of English, but received us very hospitably and insisted on our stopping to dine with him. Here, I tasted, for the first time, a real Cuban dinner. The dishes were many of them strange to me, but very palatable, and I give the Spaniards credit for the style and flavor of their dishes. The red or Catalan wine appeared to be the common beverage after being diluted with water. We stayed with Bittun between one and two hours and took horses again just before dark, and started for this place which is distant twelve or fifteen miles, but a smart ride of a couple of hours brought us here where I am at home for the present. I notice how different are the saddle horses here from ours at the north. Here they are trained for the saddle, and their gait is a march, fast and slow and called marching, for a change you can occasionally get them into a trot, or pace but their natural gait is a short trot or march, and they will go at this same gait, I am informed, for whole days with but little rest, easily making fifty miles a day, and are more hardy and enduring than our northern horses. Here they are not shod and the prevailing fashion is to cut the mane short (or braid it), and to braid up the tail fastening the end to the cantle of the saddle. The ride through the country by moonlight was truly delightful. Over broad savannahs and dark woods occasionally dashing through some village of thatched houses, raising the ire of the dogs, then riding quietly under the shadows of the stately palm and the groves of coconuts and guavas. The thickets were loaded with wild flowers, heavy with perfume. It seemed to me a ride through fairyland (always, excepting the dogs) and left an impression on my memory which can never be effaced. We kept close to the volante, which Antonio drove along at a very rapid pace, and about nine o'clk we drove up to the front gate of estate San Ricardo. Don Ricardo was ready to receive us and after an hour's chat we (or I certainly) felt tired enough to go to bed, and found myself a little the worse for wear on account of my first ride on horseback in Cuba.

Went out today to get some little idea of the operation of making sugar but shall not attempt to describe my impressions until I am better posted up. I find that eating oranges as I pick them from the trees to be very palatable exercise and the flavor of the fruit very different from what we have at the north. Bananas also taste different here, so good that it is past all my attempt at description. Finished up my day's work by going round the sugarhouse with John H. and wound up with a couple of cups of warm guarapo, or boiling juice of the cane. Its flavor is good, something similar to maple molasses. We retire early here for we rise early.

Tuesday, February 15

THE GUARAPO I drank last evening troubled me during the night with a severe pain in my barriga and I was obliged to get hold of the first stimulant I could find, and the result was I disposed of at least half a pint of my good gin. I arose early with a bad feeling head and a touch of diarrhea, but toward noon felt much better. Took a trip into the woods and cut a few canes or walking sticks, but found the underbrush rather too thick for comfortable locomotion. Life here to me is very different than at the North. We pass the day somewhat after this fashion. Rise about six o'clk and swallow a cup of coffee, brought in by Chevarro or Cora, then go out into the piazza and eat oranges just picked from the trees, then for exercise ride about the estate (on horseback of course), through the canefields, over the savannahs etc., going in all perhaps two or six miles, until about ten o'clk when breakfast is ready. For this meal we generally have fresh or salt fish, <u>tesajo</u> or jerked beef, plantains, yuca, sweet potatoes, <u>funche</u> and rice, (which is cooked no where else as here) and then yam or corn cakes, coffee and cigarettos. After breakfast go over to the sugarhouse, look at the engine grinding the cane, talk with Mr. Peck, the engineer, chew sugarcane. Then walk over to the drying and packinghouse, sometimes mark boxes of sugar, and see the carts loaded for shipping that day. Then a ride into the fields to see how the hands get along cutting cane, and by this time 'tis twelve o'clk and the sun is getting uncomfortably warm and we return to the house for a lunch of oranges, bananas or pineapples, and for a beverage take fresh coconut milk or tamarind water. By this time a short nap is desirable and can be followed by reading, writing, or other light exercise, until about four or five o'clk when we are summoned to dinner. Here we find vegetable soup of a quality which the negroes excel everybody else, duck, ham, turkey, fresh pork, etc., and occasionally a boiled dish composed of pounded plantain, meats and vegetables which is called "<u>fufu</u>" and is universal here. We have the same vegetables as in the morning with green peas, tomatoes, lettuce, beans, "<u>kim bumbo</u>" or okra, etc., cooked in every variety of style, for the negroes here are the very best of cooks. For desert we have occasionally a Yankee pudding but generally "dulces" or sweetmeats, made of guava, limes, oranges, sour sofu, tomatoes, etc., always followed by coffee and cigars. Pies and pastry are unknown here and entirely uncalled for, and fruits of every kind are about in such profusion, that they are rarely put upon the table. Everyone helping themselves in the piazza or directly from the trees. After dinner and until bedtime, we have books, papers, etc., and talk over annexation, and how much better Cuba would be if belonging to the States. During the evening we have tea or chocolate brought in and smoke cigarros, etc., until bedtime, when I take the opportunity to write for an hour or so.

Wednesday, February 16

THIS ESTATE I am informed is a small one being about one mile in extent each way, but every available piece of land well stocked with cane. It is like nearly all others, laid out in a circle one mile in diameter, the intervening land being waste, or belonging to the government. It is situated near the great savannah, De La Palma, which is scarcely cultivated. The number of slaves here is about one hundred in all, men, women, and children, and about a dozen hired Creoles, and the number of boxes of sugar produced about 2,000. Some of the larger estates have a much greater number of slaves and make much more sugar. One, the estate of San Martin about three leagues from here, has bout 1,500 hands and makes annually about

25,000 boxes of sugar, the average price of which is about $18 a box, so the gross receipts of the estate will amount to at least $450,000, and the profits on this are at least twenty percent. You see that sugar making is a lucrative business. When the crop is a good one, as it is this year being unusually large and the prices well up.

The shooting is good in this vicinity, we have close by a pond full of a variety of ducks, and in the woods close by are plenty of quails, partridges and pigeons. The guinea fowls of which there are great numbers about here, we treat as game being too wild to catch otherwise when wanted for the table.

There are two kinds of marked lands on the island, the red, and the black lands. The red is a species of sandy clay, almost of our dark brick color, and much dryer than the black. In a moist winter like this one the red lands do the best. It is understood that tobacco and coffee do best on the red lands and sugar on the black, but on this place which is red land I find <u>everything</u> grows rapidly. The sugarcane now being cut measures from twelve to fifteen feet in height and is round and full. I notice here among the different varieties of trees, growing here, the mahogany, palm, cedar, copaiba, India rubber ceiba, bamboo, pimento, pepper, mango, breadfruit, coconut, orange, lemon, tamarind, caimito (a species of plum), aguacate (or alligator pear), and many others that I can find no English name to correspond. Of fruits there are an endless variety, many of which are never seen in the northern states, such as mango, sapota, sweet lemon, guanabana, citron, bananas, maranox, pineapple, toronja (or orange), guava, etc. Cotton also grows here wild, and a fine quality is being cultivated which is called the green seed of Chinese cotton, and said to be nearly or quite equal to the far famed "sea island cotton." Coffee, indigo, vanilla, and tonquin beans grow wild, and are cultivated to some extent, but it is evident to anyone that the resources of the island are not half developed. With proper culture it would be the tropical market of the world.

The island is not only rich in vegetable products but also in minerals. Gold and silver were in early times found in considerable quantities, and copper now abounds throughout the island. Iron, plumbago, copperas and antimony can easily be obtained. Coal is plenty but not of good quality as yet being softer than that of our western states. There are already extensive quarries of marble and limestone. The color of the latter is a light cream, nearly white, and when first taken out, is soft and brittle and can easily be cut with a hatchet, but becomes hard and firm by exposure to air and is generally now used for building purposes in the cities.

Mineral springs of great sanative power are in various parts of the island, and Cuba bids fair yet to rival Saratoga, Sharon or the Virginia Sulpher springs. The climate is very uniform, the thermometer rarely ranges above 90° in the hottest season or below 60° in the winter. When at 60° the Havaneros complain of cold, and overcoats are in demand. Snow has never been seen on the island, and fires are never needed (except for cooking, etc.). The nights are always cool, a blanket being needed even in the hottest season. The northeast wind here is cool and refreshing, and the wind is from this quarter nearly all of the winter season. A southerly wind brings heat and foretells rain, and is generally followed by a <u>norther</u> or cold storm of wind and rain. There are many more days of cloudy and partially cloudy days here than at the North, which tend to mitigate the heat, and protect from the scorching rays of the sun.

I am indebted to Thrasher's translation of Humboldt's *Cuba* for many statistics and to these I combine information received from reliable friends and a little practical personal observation. I see something new and strange to me, and worthy of notice everyday.

The clearness and beauty of the sky is beyond all description, and its effects upon the life and luxuriant growth of vegetation is proportionate. A high temperature moderated by great evaporation, caused by the heavy dews, conduces to rapid growth, and thus it is through all seasons of the year, the fields and forests of Cuba perceive their verdure, and it is said that at the commencement of summer, or rainy season, all nature seems transformed to flowers. To notice the rapid growth, I took a plantain tree planted last Sunday morning, a slip, and find by actual measurement the average growth is just three inches every twenty-four hours, and this in poor land without any artificial stimulant.

In clearing new lands for planting sugarcane, etc., the trees are felled, and what are not required for fuel, are left to rot on the ground, and such is the humidity of the atmosphere, and the heat of the sun, that in two years the wood entirely decays, and the soil is ready for plowing and planting.

Thursday, February 17

I LEARN that there are Americans in all parts of the island, and the number permanently located here last year was estimated at twenty-five hundred, mostly employed as machinists and mechanics, though there are quite a number of planters and administrators on estates who are Americans. Those employed here get good wages, a competent and capable engineer gets $120 a month during the grinding season lasting about six months, and carpenters $60 to $75 per month through the year, and for both board and lodging included. A carpenter here must turn his hand to anything in the mending line, from shingling a house to moving a chair or ox cart. The great majority of the planters are Creoles, and the Spaniards are nearly all office holders or traders. In the army no Cubans are admitted, and this adds 40,000 alone to the Spanish population. They are raised by conscription, but money always buys a substitute in old Spain, consequently they nearly all belong to the very lowest class of Spanish peasantry and have no feeling in common with the Creoles, who they hate most cordially and I believe the feeling is reciprocal. Many of the army officers are gentlemen of education and intelligence, and have travelled over a great portion of Europe, perhaps, speak several languages, are polite and attentive to strangers, but they very rarely speak our language, and show a remarkable ignorance of everything connected with the United States, of our extent, commerce, and general disposition, they have very crude ideas. The lower class of Spaniards do really believe that the United States is less in geographical extent than this island, that our people are but hardly an advance on the aboriginals, that we have no army or military force, and no navy at all, but that we occasionally borrow a frigate from the English to show off at Havana. They fully believe themselves able at anytime to land an army and take possession of the "Estados Unidos."

The whole income derived from this island to the crown of Spain is about eighteen million of dollars by taxation in various forms, of which about eight million only goes to the home government, the balance being used for the payment of officials (item the Captain General receives a salary of $50,000 per annum) and for the support of the army and navy stationed here. There is a very large force here besides the regular army of whom I have spoken. They are styled the volunteers ("los voluntarios") and are uniformed and equipped the same as the regular army. They are composed of the Spanish residents and perform the police duty of the island, and are stationed all over the country, for one cannot ride on the main road for half a dozen miles without meeting some of them. If we are considered suspicious or look like <u>filibusteros</u> the officer in command satisfies his consequence by a look at your travelling license, and the common soldiers look ferocious, and if you wear good clothes, look somewhat avaricious. They all <u>look</u> as if a dollar would buy their souls. In meeting a Spaniard of your acquaintance, a great palaver is necessary, for as a people they make a great many words over a small matter and go into the <u>details</u> of everything, but they do give us lessons in politeness, for on meeting one is always saluted with "<u>Buenas dias, Señor</u>," and on parting with "<u>Adios, Señor</u>."

The *New York Herald*, so radically <u>democratic</u> and red republican in its ideas generally, is sometimes prohibited in its circulation on the island, and now, there is a disposition not to give it a chance to be read to any extent, as many copies I have sent here have never reached their destination. Still stray copies do penetrate every portion of the island, and just now especially do those relating to congressional proceedings, relative to the thirty million project get passed about from hand to hand. The late debates in Congress in regard to annexation or purchase of Cuba, the action of the Democratic State Convention, and the speeches in the mass meeting at New Rochelle relative to the acquisition of Cuba, as reported by the last files of the *Herald* have been read pretty generally by the Creoles, and if some of our politicians at the North could know the <u>real</u> feelings and aspirations of the Cubans they <u>might</u> change their opinions as to the <u>real</u> sentiments of the people of Cuba.

Friday, February 18

A SUGAR PLANTATION is called an estate (Ingenio—pronounced yenhanyo) and the number of boxes of sugar produced is proportionate to the number of hands employed. This estate is a small one comparatively and owns about one hundred negroes of all kinds and produces annually some two thousand boxes of sugar (this includes in the estimate the muscovada sugar and molasses). The cane is ready for cutting about the middle of December, and it is continued until all is cut, generally finishing about the first of May. It is cut just as fast as can be ground and no great amount is left cut and waiting to be ground at any time. The cane does not require planting except where old and worn lands are broken up to be re-worked, and it is not hoed as formerly, but ploughed through with a cultivator. A few days after being cut the new cane commences springing up, so the first cutting this year is the first ready for cutting next season. The cutting of the cane is done by the negroes of both sexes, with a long heavy knife called a <u>machete,</u> and the stalks only are put upon the cart to be carried to the mill; the leaves and tops are left upon the field and answer the purpose of manure, except the portion saved for food of the horses and cattle on the place, of which they are very fond, preferring it to corn leaves. Good land lasts for twenty years or more without ploughing, or any artificial manures. The cane is brought to the mill in huge carts, and the grinding is performed by means of a steam engine, which after pressing the juice from the stalk throws off the refuse, which is called <u>bagasse</u>, and this after being dried in the sun, constitutes the fuel for fires to boil the juice. The boiler is heated by wood of which there is an abundance on the surrounding hills. The juice is run into huge pans set over a long range or furnace, and then boiled down and passed from one pan to another, till it acquires the proper consistence and is then dipped into tanks to cool. (While boiling, the negroes beat it with long wooden paddles, and sing a kind of medley and chant, which is peculiar to the sugarhouse. I could hardly make out the words but it sounded like, "<u>a—a cha candala e bla—ebla fuerte—echa candala</u>," etc., etc., which is a cry to the firemen to put on more heat, more fire, etc. This monotonous chant is heard without intermission day and night for the negro cannot work without talking or singing and each new gang take up the same song. After the boiled syrup is partly cooled it is poured into iron cones or tubes to <u>purge</u> and packed over with clay to whiten. The molasses is drained through from these tubes and carried off by troughs into a large tank, these to be put into hogsheads. The sugar is carried to the drying house, and when sufficiently cured in the sun, is packed up in boxes and ready for shipping. (These boxes are mostly made in New England and cost here $1 each.) Each box contains from 450 to 500 lbs. and is sold by the box at prices varying with the demand. The average price is about $20 a box. The muscovada or brown sugar is not purged or whitened, and is packed in hogsheads weighing from 1000 to 2000 lbs. each and this sells from $1.00 to $1.50 per <u>arroba</u> or 25¢ according to quality. About 300 hogsheads are made here annually, and also about 300 hogsheads of molasses each year, which is taken from the tanks by the distiller at about $12 per hogshead. Some idea may be formed of the quantity of saccharin fluid in the cane, when I say it requires about 500 gallons of cane juice to make one box of sugar, so there are on this place boiled up every year one million gallons of juice.

During the grinding season the negroes are divided into two gangs, in order to work all night, and to avoid the want of fresh hands, changing at midnight. Every ten days or so the grinding is stopped for two or three days, to give an opportunity to clean the pans, boiler and engine and to give the hands rest. While at work the negroes are continually singing their African melodies and keeping time by beating the boiling sugar of which I believe I have just spoken. They are well treated, and well fed, but as to clothing it is difficult to keep much of anything like clothing on them during the day. They seem contented and if they get enough to eat and occasionally a cigar to smoke they rarely complain. They are constitutionally indolent, and have no more judgement than an animal, consequently there are always some in the hospital. With a good owner (the one here is too indulgent, I think) whipping is rare, but the most common punishment is placing in the stocks for a few hours, or solitary confinement in the calaboose, and fed on bread and water. The negro dreads being alone, and craves companionship, food, etc. When the owner of an estate lives abroad, the whole is under charge of an agent called "administrador." There are also employed on the estate, an engineer, carpenter, a mayoral or overseer, a majordomo or clerk and first and second sugar masters. There are also under drovers, etc., and generally negroes, and these are the most tyranical and cruel of all others. The engineer and carpenter are generally Americans and the others guajiros or natives of the island.

Quite a large portion of this estate (San Ricardo) is cultivated for plantains, yuca, yams, sweet potatoes, corn and rice, as food for the family and the slaves, and another portion for the portreros or pastures for horses, cattle and sheep, but yet I can look out of my window toward the savannahs and see canefields of half a mile in extent. After seeing the way molasses is made, one can hardly have a fancy to taste it, but it is presumed that fermentation cleans and purifies it thoroughly. Here the sugar syrup, or fresh boiled juice unfermented called malow [melado] is used for the table and for cooking.

The boiling juice of the cane called guarapo is a favorite drink with the Creoles, and combined with a little old rum makes a very palatable punch, as I can testify from experience.

Tonight about ten o'clk Vincente d'Larallette and Ned Wilson came up from Cardenas, of course we were glad to meet and talked over matters until twelve o'clk. They brought along with them a proclamation of the Lieutenant Governor of Cardenas. The pomposity of some of the Spanish officials and the verbose style of language used in such proclamations, etc., seemed quite laughable to me, and I induced Ned to translate the heading for me and have made a note of it. The proclamation was issued regarding some audacious highway robberies, lately committed, giving warning to all good and evil disposed persons, relating all the pains and penalties in seven different articles, all signed and sealed by him and posted on all stores and public places within his official district. I have a copy of the proclamation before me and copy a literal translation of the heading printed in big type, giving the titles, etc., of said Lieutenant Governor who issues the proclamation: "Don Bruno Gayosa, gentleman of the Royal Military order of Saint Hermanegildo, Benefactor of the Country, Colonel alive and effective of Infantry, Military commander and Lieut. Governor of this District; sub-delegate of the Royal Treasury; President of the Municipal Council; and of the Jurisdictional Council of Public Works, and of the Board of Health; of Primary Schools; of the Council of Charity; Judge Protector of the Royal Income of Lotteries and of the Post Office, etc., etc." Titles go a great way in this country, and although a simple minded Yankee, may rest satisfied as a Justice of the Peace, the ambitious Spaniard never tires of adding new honors to his name, in the shape of titles, etc.

Wrote several letters today, among others several to friends at home. Also fourth one to *Hartford Times* for publication having written three previously (two in Havana).

Saturday, February 19

Q UITE WARM today, but not uncomfortable as my friend John has <u>quantum sufficit</u> of thin clothing and invites me to make free with his wardrobe, which I do without ceremony. We have all been over to the <u>tabernas</u> today, which is a little shop or tavern about half a mile from the house, where is kept for sale a little of everything. To-morrow is mail day and a steamer having arrived at Havana I expect letters from home, and advices concerning baggage which is I hope in Havana by this time. Wrote to Burr fifth letter for *Times* today.

The <u>tabernas</u> are shops kept all along the public roads, every few miles we meet one, and they are always kept by Catalans or Spaniards. They prefer the work of the counter to all others, and I have not as yet seen a single Spaniard cultivating the soil. This seems strange considering the general (assumed) dignified character of the Spanish race, because the business of the taverner requires great patience and forbearance, as they sometimes suffer the most degrading humiliations even from negroes. But for money it seems they will do <u>almost</u> anything; and it is a Creole proverb, that every Spaniard can be bought. I think this belief is held among the Spaniards themselves and thus their anxiety and worry about the passage of the thirty million bill. The debate and feeling manifested in the United States has already done good here for the tone of the Spaniards toward "<u>los Yan-</u>

kees" has been greatly mollified within a few weeks past.

Sunday, February 20

EARLY THIS MORNING Joe Wilson arrived from his place, forty miles further up country, having started at three o'clk and come down in four hours or so. A morning ride of thirty or forty miles is not considered a great deal here, of course, he came on horseback. We have now here five of the party who were together in Bristol last summer. We have a fine time today talking over old affairs. The seven who are not here (viz Ed and William Fales, William Roberts, William Dimock, Dr. Budd Rogers D'Wolf, and Ned Wheaton) were not forgotten. Vincente devoted a great portion of his time to Anita but the rest of us walked and talked almost all day. The correo (postman) brought me letters from William Dimock and William Roberts and from home and, of course, this made me happy. Also we received files of the *New York Herald* which was eagerly scanned, and all the news relating to Cuba, the thirty million bill, etc., etc., was read aloud by Ned. We passed the whole day together. Ned and Vincente going off about ten o'clk this evening by moonlight, but well armed.

A stranger here if he be at all modest, is somewhat shocked by one peculiarity, which he sees the first hour he lands upon this island, whether in city or country, in houses, in the streets and in fact everywhere. The young negroes of both sexes (and in many cases young Spaniards too) under the age of about ten years, are accustomed to go about in a perfect state of nudity and the men of the same classes, who performed street labor, wear pantaloons, as the only covering to the body, displaying their brawny muscles at every moment. On the plantations the slaves of both sexes wear hardly clothes enough to make them appear decently. The intense heat of the summer to those exposed to field labor is the excuse given for this, and all the clothing a real guinea or congo negro desires to wear in the field is a broad palm leaf hat. The more intelligent sometimes wear a cloth wrapped around the loins and a fancy colored handkerchief twisted about the head. The "Georgia Colonel" whose uniform consisted of a <u>shirt collar and spurs</u>, would be totally eclipsed here.

Monday, February 21

IT IS NECESSARY for a stranger coming to the island, who indulges in smoking, to understand two words of Spanish at the outset. One is <u>candela</u>, a light (or <u>fuego, fire</u>) and the other <u>gracias</u>, thank you. You hear these words continually, and as a great many here smoke cigarillos (or cigarros as they are called here), they have the more occasion for a light. The Spaniards as I have said before I think, have an outward show of great politeness, and on entering and leaving a store, always you bid the proprietor a good day, etc. If you visit the house of a Don, or even a Creole, he first informs you that his "house is at your disposal," the same also if you admire any article of his property, though he means nothing of the kind, and the expression may be considered as equivalent to "make yourself at home," etc., of the English language.

It is estimated that the number of Spaniards living on the island is from eighty to one hundred thousand souls without including the army and navy. The expense of emigration, the fear of yellow fever, and the uncertainty of getting good situations, keep the yearly emigration down to a small figure, not withstanding the probabilities of making a fortune. They generally come over from Spain, at the instance of relatives already here, and the general appearance and manners of a great portion of them, gives a very poor idea of the civilization of the mother country, and even the negroes here seem to look down upon them. The inferiority of the lower classes of Spain, when compared with those of Cuba, is even acknowledged by the Spaniards themselves. They may be seen by the cartload, the same as we see the very poorest class of emigrants coming up from Castle Garden in New York, and their appearance is very similar. They stare about, wondering at everything they see, and are pictures of filth, hunger and nakedness. They are called "sucios blancos" (dirty whites) by the negroes and yet shortly after landing these wretches consider themselves masters of the country, and assume a superiority over the Creoles. They keep steadily in view the prospect of making a fortune, from the highest government official, down to the lowest Catalan fresh from the Penninsula. It is a remarkable fact that those coming to this country throw off their idleness, which is characteristic of their nation, and here become industrious and very economical. Those who are not employed by government (and their name is <u>legion</u>), devote themselves to trade, and when as clerks or servants, they have amassed a little capital, they are ready to undertake any kind of trade or speculation from selling rum to negroes, to a dash into the slave trade. They sometimes become <u>refaccionistas</u> (or those who sell the crops for the planters and make advances of goods and money) without anything much more than nominal capital, and by charging usurious interest, making false entries, etc., they swell the account so large, that not unfrequently in a few years they find themselves owners of the estates they have been supplying; and then they endeavor to marry some rich lady and finally purchase a title or crop of distinction, for they can be had of all grades and prices, and go back to old Spain a <u>grandee</u>.

The Spanish nobility has many just such sprigs among them. There is a druggist on Matanzas whose portrait I have seen who wears a gorgeous uniform and has his breast covered with crosses and orders and yet all these are bought and paid for, as he never performed a single day's military duty or served his country any way, except in the way of pills, powders, etc. There is a marquis in Havana who within the last twenty years commenced his career as a gate or door keeper, which is considered a very inferior and humble occupation. He finally succeeded in marrying the daughter of a wealthy Portuguese (<u>a la Baker and Dean</u>)

though strongly opposed by the father. He bought his title of marquis and the cross of honor, of St. Hermanegildo, and aspiring to an office in the army bought the commission of colonel. He now rides about in his carriage attended by a crowd of servitors and may often be seen at the opera in full uniform with his breast covered with glittering orders, though I can safely assert he has never carried a musket or wielded a sword in defense of the crown. I have been told of a number of similar cases and there is no question of the truth of it.

I do not mean to say that all the Spanish nobility are composed of such for there are those who date back their ancestry to the early days of Spanish glory and not a few have unmistakable marks of Moorish blood in their veins. The Count Fernandina is a Spanish nobleman of great wealth and importance, and has a very dignified personal appearance which would anywhere command respect. The Countess is a pale faced delicate looking woman, universally admired and beloved, and she is said to be almost a "filibustero" in her views as to manifest destiny. Certain it is she is very partial to the Americanos. They have a magnificent place out on the Cerro a couple of miles outside the walls, and on my return to Havana, if possible, I shall have a look at it. There are many grandees of Spain who are descended from Irish families and descendants of Irishmen who entered the Spanish service after the unsuccessful rebellion of 1798. O'Donnell, O'Landor, O'Reilly, and O'Farrel, and many others and their successors rank high in the Spanish court.

Enough of the nobility now. Joe Wilson returned home to his estate <u>Nueva Esperanza</u> (New Hope) this afternoon and we have promised to visit him before my return.

Tuesday, February 22

WROTE SIXTH LETTER to *Times* today. Washington's Birthday, but no celebrations here. They honor any quantity of saints days, as ordered by the head of the Catholic Church, and the birthdays of Queen Isabel and her numerous progeny. It is estimated that about one-third of all the days of the year, are <u>holy days</u> and on such, no official business is transacted.

It is evident to any observer here that the Creoles and Spaniards live together as cats and dogs would if locked up in the same cage. A Creole speaking of the Spanish character says "Spaniards are haughty towards the humble, and humble towards the haughty; courageous with the cowards, and cowards with the courageous." So far as I am able to judge this description contains as much truth as poetry. The Spaniards in Cuba possess many advantages over the Creoles for becoming wealthy. The government affords them a decided protection, though it professes great impartiality. Besides the offices, which are wholly monopolized by the Spaniards, many highly profitable contracts with the exchequer, and "fat jobs" in general are awarded to them on the most advantageous terms. It is worth noticing, however, that but few Spaniards employ their countrymen for lawyers or physicians and that they prefer Creoles. Persons emigrating from Spain, if they are of the legal profession, solicit judicial offices, and if they are physicians, request the judges to appoint them to commissions, to enable them to gain a respectable position, for the public greatly distrust the capacities of these adventurers. I heard of a quarrel between a Spanish tavern keeper and a free negro. They disputed about the weight of some article purchased and the negro charged the Spaniard with cheating him. The negro uttered all kinds of hard and insulting epithets which the philosophical (or cowardly) storekeeper bore with great patience, and tried to soothe and pacify the negro, but without showing any disposition to make restitution. Among other insulting and opprobious epithets he emphasized the word "<u>Catalan,</u>" plainly showing that he considered it one of the most insulting of names.

Wednesday, February 23

R ODE OVER to <u>Teneria,</u> a neighboring estate about 2 miles below us on the road. It is quite a large one having between three and four hundred hands, and everything looks neat and trim there. The owner of the estate is the Marquis Morales who resides in Havana, and has never even <u>seen</u> this place. He owns several other estates in different parts of the island, but leaves the management entirely in the hands of agents. He is also the owner of very large tracts of land in this vicinity, much of it improved, on which the occupants pay him tribute. I have not heard his income estimated but it must be immense.

The roads on the island are generally very bad, and no pains are taken to remedy the fault. During the rainy season they are almost impassable, except for horses, and in the dry season the roads are full of deep ruts and holes. There are but very few bridges, and most of the creeks and rivers have to be forded, which is sometimes a dangerous experiment to one not thoroughly acquainted with the crossings. The banks are generally lined with soft heavy mud or clay, that would permanently set a wheeled vehicle, were any place but just the right one selected for crossing; and indeed it is so bad, even at this season that cattle frequently while grazing on the savannahs go to the creek for water, and accidentally become fast in the mud, and unless they get assistance, soon sink down and die there. I have seen more than one such a case myself. The carcass is completely disposed of by turkey buzzards within twenty-four hours generally. The badness of the road is perhaps in part owing to the clumsy build of the carts used in carting sugar and molasses. They are huge wooden frames, which, when empty, three men can scarcely move. The great strength given to them may be necessary to withstand the shocks and concussions to which they are continually liable. Their own weight, however, prevents easy motion, forms deep ruts and constitutes the principal cause of the destruction of the roads. I should judge that these unwieldy carts cannot weigh less than one ton each, and as the regular load carried by them is eight boxes of sugar, or about thirty-eight hundred pounds, it requires, on a level road, three yoke of oxen to propel it. Three or four of these teams generally go together, and when one gets into a deep rut, the other teams must take hold and help him out. The cartmen (<u>carreteros</u>) are generally <u>guajiros</u> or countrymen, and their life is one of hardship, and they are not well paid. In the rainy season they are covered with mud, and wet through as often as once in twenty-four hours, and then heated during the day by the intense rays of a tropical sun. They hang a hammock under the cart, and sleep there with a sombrero over the face for protection against mosquitoes and thus they go for days at a time without taking off their clothes, and without any stimulating drink except strong coffee. They are a strong, hardy set, and though generally undersized men, seem capable of enduring great hardship. They are ignorant and rough in their ways, yet they affect superiority over the Spanish taverner, and often abuse him soundly for endeavoring to cheat them, which he bears with philosophical calmness, feeling undoubtedly that the <u>dinero</u> (money) is an equivalent for hard words.

Thursday, February 24

S TARTED AT about noon today for <u>Sabinilla de la Palma</u>. <u>Enroute</u> for Cardenas, John and myself accompanied by "<u>Chevarro</u>" (a black boy) to take charge of our horses etc., for no one rides or travels here without a negro attendant. He follows on a packhorse and carries our carpetbags, etc., with

him. We go armed, of course, for no one travels
for any distance here on the roads without being
prepared for any kind of difficulty. We stopped at
Hato Nuevo for a little time to call on the Capitan
d'Partido, Don Pasquale, to pay our respects to
his wife, and her sister Señorita Ellena Hermanez.
We stopped at the taverns to rest occasionally for
the afternoon was very warm and then came to
the village or depot of Sabinilla de la Palma, a collection of a store, blacksmith's shop, depot, and
three or four palm covered dwellings. We had to
attend to the forwarding of some sugar, etc., here
for this [is] a termination of the branch of the
(Ferro Carril) railroad running from Cardenas and
distant about twelve miles from San Ricardo. From
here we rode over to Santa Catalina some three or
four miles where we proposed to dine with our
friend Bittun. We visited his sugarhouse, inspected
his engine and he showed me personally much
attention. I was also personally indebted to his
slave Victoria (a fine plump mulatto) for a delicious basket of fruit. Bittun is a good administrator but they say a perfect brute among the niggers.
I saw him knock down a girl with his cane for some
trifling matter about his horse's bridle. We stayed
all night and retired early as we had become somewhat fatigued with our afternoon's work.

Friday, February 25

U P EARLY this morning, and off before breakfast (after coffee and cigars of course) for the
Recreo depot some two or three miles from Santa

Catalina. Here we took the cars and arrived at Cardenas about ten o'clk. We breakfasted at eleven at the lonca [lonja] (or exchange) on several rich dishes. One dish composed of calf's brains served up with asparagus, a dish of rice and eggs, cakes of yam, etc., etc., with a couple of bottles of excellent [. . .] wine. After shaving, hair cutting, etc., we had considerable shopping to attend to and I bought myself a sombrero, and as I have tanned up well, I can readily pass for a Creole. I find my trunk and carpet bag deposited by the express at Safford and Co. counting room and take pleasure in finding everything correct except some few trifling things which I suppose were taken as kind of toll on the way. The whole amount of expense on them from New York is about fourteen dollars. In the afternoon we visited the old cemetery where George D'Wolf was buried, and toward evening we took a volante for Esperanza (Mr. Fortun's estate) about five miles out of the city. Mr. and Mrs. F. were returning from Matanzas and reached home shortly after we arrived. We also met here Charles and Edward Wilson, and after dinner spent a pleasant evening. Charles W. and myself played chess and John and Ed amused themselves by drinking Mr. Fortun's excellent Spanish white wine. John and Ed rode over to Charles W.'s place to spend the night and I retired about ten o'clk. Mr. Fortun's house is of a superior class to most of the residences in this country and furnished very prettily. His wife being an American lady, shows native taste in fitting up, etc., and her table has a variety of both Spanish and American dishes.

Saturday, February 26

U P EARLY looking about the Esperanza and after breakfast about ten o'clk, rode into Cardenas with Mr. Fortun. As he speaks but <u>very</u> little
English and I as little Spanish, our conversation
was necessarily somewhat restricted, but both
being of a sociable turn we managed to get along.
He showed me the better portion of Cardenas and
some fine residences in the upper part of the city.
Afterward I called at his office (Pell Cantera y Co.)
and made the acquaintance of several merchants,
etc. Met John and Ned toward noon and we
lunched etc., together. We met also with Mr. Nellis,
the no-armed man who has just arrived from the
states, and who proposes to astonish the Car-
denese with his performances after the carnival.
At three o'clk we take the cars for Recreo, and on
the way to the depot we persuade Ned to go up
with us and spend the night at Bittun's. On arriving at Recreo we find Domingo waiting for us with
horses. On our way up we had considerable fun
with a mettlesome Spaniard who showed more
than ordinary national stupidity. I opened a pack-
age of New York Sunday weeklies, pictorial papers, etc., which I had taken out from my
carpetbag, and found folded in one, a printed slip
or handbill of a Broadway merchant, offering Cen-
tral Park <u>skates</u> at reduced prices, etc. The idea of
<u>such</u> an advertisement in <u>this</u> climate was so ri-
diculous that I showed it to Ned and we laughed
over it, sticking it in my hat band. The <u>Don</u> sitting
opposite (apparently an intelligent man too)

looked at me very seriously for some time and finally said to Ned, "Advise your friend to take that from his sombrero or he will get into trouble." We all laughed and explained what it meant—an advertisement for <u>skates</u> and what skates were used for, etc., but he said he knew all about it and there was no use of our trying to humbug him. He knew skates were used in Holland, but not in the United States, and although he pretended to be able to read English, he said it might <u>read</u> skates but it had a double meaning that it <u>meant</u> war, and was a proclamation from Buchanan, and if it was not removed from my hat, he would take it off himself. At this Ned bristled up and they had some sharp conversation and ended by Ned taking him roughly by the shoulders and forcing him into his own seat and showing him <u>ten</u> commandments, doubled up into the shape of a big pair of fists, and told him if he touched my hat he would annihilate him. The <u>brave</u> Spaniard immediately cooled down and apologized, which drew a laugh upon him from several English and American passengers, which irritated the Don again, and he said "there were too many Americans here already, and they were coming so fast and wouldn't wait for the thirty millions, etc." He left us at the Pelego station, threatening to complain to the Captain General and also to the Queen if necessary to have all these d_d Americans driven from the island.

We dine with Bittun and sit up late talking over old times at the North and smoking cigars, under the piazza. The houses here are all one story high, with piazza running nearly all around it, shaded with climbing vines, and thickets of roses, oleanders and jasmine. The night air was heavy with the perfume of a splendid nightblooming jasmine and there we sat and watched the stars as they glistened through this paradise of fruit and flowers. Here were southern roses, altheas, and cactus shrubs of magnificent proportions, all growing with but little care. The days for the last week have been clear and warm and the nights cool and serene, the air pure and elastic and the results, are there are no colds and coughs here, such a country for an invalid, it is almost a paradise.

Wrote to Dora before retiring.

Sunday, February 27

WE RETIRED late, for the night was a little warmer than usual at this season, a south wind having prevailed through the day, but I could not sleep for my mind was far away, among my friends at home and imagining how they were now and how differently we were situated, for a warm night in the tropics is very different from a summer night at the North. There the silence may occasionally be broken by the crowing of the cock, the bark of a dog or the forte notes of a feline domestic, but here as soon as the sun sinks beneath the glowing horizon, the air is all alive with sounds. We have here the "go back, go back" of the guinea fowl, the "twee twee" of the lizard and the sweet song of the peacock at regular intervals. The night breeze sighs mournfully, and insects go humming and droning about; the little knocker, knocks, the [. . .] chirps loudly, and <u>tree frogs,</u> <u>mosquitoes</u> and <u>sand flies</u> all vie with each other in exhibiting their musical developments, and there is no peace. "Gentlemen may cry peace, peace, but there is <u>no</u> peace." The insect world is in a state of frantic revelry and to try and accompany them, one would get into a fury and perhaps a fever. This perhaps induced me to rise early and I was rewarded by having a fine view of that splendid constellation the "Southern Cross," shining brightly, just above the southern horizon. We started for home early, and after a cup of delicious coffee and lighting our cigars, while our horses were getting ready we strolled out into the garden, but the ground was so damp from the heavy dew that my feet soon became wet, but the balmy fragrance from all the plants, and especially of the flowers of the garden (which was at the same time an orange grove), afforded such pleasure as I think I never before experienced. The trees were in full bearing and recalled to mind what we are told of the garden of Hesperides. It was a beautiful sight and the odor from the new orange blossoms was almost oppressively sweet. It is not till one eats oranges plucked fresh from the trees that he becomes aware of the delightful relish of the fruit. It is very different from the fruit we buy for "fresh Havana oranges" in New York. Here we leave Ned W.

We have a smart ride of some fifteen miles to San Ricardo and arrived in season for breakfast, for these little Creole horses easily <u>march</u> eight or ten miles an hour, and a morning ride of fifteen miles is thought a short one; and the motion of the horse so very easy, one soon becomes accustomed to it, and a ride of this distance is not as fatiguing as a canter or trot of a couple of miles on our northern horses.

The <u>correo</u> brought me today several letters and papers from home and I forwarded several that I had written for friends at home and in New York. I find by home papers that the affair of Doctor Brocket's forgery and Sam Jones' arrest for Colchester Bank fraud are the only topics discussed in Connecticut though politics <u>are warming</u> up in view of election which comes off [the] first [of] April.

Monday, February 28

WHEN IN HAVANA I witnessed a kind of military funeral which was anything but solemn or imposing. First came the hearse, a large lumbering car, ornamented with a profusion of black plumes and drapery, drawn by a dozen black horses, each led by a negro, and the hearse driver on an elevated seat, ridiculously dressed up and surmounted by a chapeau and black feathers. Next came a platoon of infantry led by a couple of officers, and a couple of drummers, pounding away as if their very life depended on the amount of noise made. Then came the <u>hired</u> mourners (for the immediate family and friends do not attend), with handkerchiefs to their eyes, and a long crape streaming from their hats, followed by about a hundred volantes of which almost every other one carried a <u>padre</u>. Ned was with me and he remarked it would cost a large sum for so many priests to say Mass, etc., but that the deceased having so many was probably some distinguished character or great rogue and probably needed a greater amount of praying to ensure his future quiet. I noticed one custom which deserves commendation. Wherever the funeral procession passed, pedestrians reverently uncovered their heads, and many signed themselves with the cross.

Wrote seventh letter for *Times* and, in the evening, the ninth letter. The last day of winter (and the thermometer 83° at noon), I can hardly realize it for it is apparently the warmest day I have seen on the island. The thermometer stands among the eighties in the shade, and although a fresh breeze is blowing this afternoon it is from the south and this always brings heat. I can imagine friends at home <u>sleighing</u>, wrapped up in buffalo robes and overcoats while here we retire to the house to avoid the heat of the sun and lay off in the thinnest of linen clothing. Rode down to Hato Nuevo this morning with John in the gig to call on the captain. I do not fancy this mode of travelling but prefer going on horseback. Returned in time for breakfast. Wrote some half dozen letters home today and ninth one for the *Times*. We took a bath today in the <u>Rio del Palma</u> (the river of Palms) and it was delicious. The clear cool water and gravelly bottom of the river produced a sensation unequalled in this warm country.

While in Havana, I noticed many things of which I haven't had time to speak. Some of the every day habits and customs of the people are so different from what we are accustomed to seeing at the North, that it naturally attracts the attention of a stranger.

The fashionable hour for making calls in the cities is just after dark. In the parlors and on a line with the sides of the large iron barred windows, are placed a double row of rocking and easy chairs facing each other. A piece of carpet or matting is sometimes placed under and in front of the chairs, but this is the only covering for the floor, which is generally tiled or cemented, and covered with a heavy coating of wax which gives it a smooth and glossy appearance. The ladies generally kiss each other, and shake hands with their gentlemen acquaintances and then chat about the opera, dancing, riding on the paseo, etc., but there is less said about "what she wore" and that sort of thing, than we generally hear at the North. The Cuban ladies show their weakness in jewelry, which is worn in great profusion, and their taste is generally for high colors in dress, but as their clothing is necessarily thin, they do not indulge in expensive silk, shawls, etc., and I presume there is less complaint of nothing to wear. Bonnets are not worn at all, so that luxury is dispensed with, but the magnificent lace veils worn in their place must cost quite or nearly as much. Every lady carries a fan, some of very elaborate workmanship, and they handle them in a style hardly to be imitated, for in fact a great portion of the flirting here is done with a fan. The gentlemen present during the call smoke if they feel so disposed, as the ladies find no fault with it, for a great many of them smoke cigarros at home, and I have seen some who were dressed as ladies riding in a volante, and puffing away at their cigars. (In the country 'tis a common occurrence to see the women among the ordinary people smoking long and strong plantation cigars.) When the ladies signify they are willing to end the visit, some one of the gentlemen present must offer his arm to the eldest and escort them to the volante, where he receives in return some complimentary expression for his polite attention and adios, accompanied with a quiet little flirt of the fan. The ladies here always ride about the streets of Havana, and though American ladies will disregard the custom, they do it at the risk of being insulted not only by the odorous filthy negroes, (the very worst class of which are the free negroes in Havana) but also by the Spaniards, who wear the clothing of, and profess to be gentlemen. They think they have a right to address a lady whom they have never seen before, and to say to her, "How handsome you are" or "I am greatly in love with you," etc., etc. This is a Spanish custom, and in the cities of old Spain, a lady considers herself slighted, if in passing a crowd of men she does not receive from them some flattering or endearing expression, and these Catalans bring this custom to Havana, where I regret to say the Cuban ladies do not receive them with the contempt and indignation they deserve. Occasionally an American lady who understands the language resents these liberties, and the case has been known where her cavalier has taught the Spaniard a lesson with his cane.

There is one peculiar custom here not found elsewhere, I think. It is courting at the window. Where the suitor is not admitted to the house on

account of not having had an introduction, or
where the girls' parents disapprove the acquaintance, she finds means for an interview. Young
ladies are not allowed to go out, except in company with a <u>duenna</u>, and so they have no opportunity of communicating in public with their
lovers, so the admirer posts himself at the window which is nearly on a level with the street, and
projecting from the house, and <u>here</u> he <u>makes love</u>
through the bars. If he is likely to be interrupted,
she gives him notice and he retires to the next
house or the adjoining corner till she gives him
the signal to come forward to the window. Their
communications are most generally verbal, for I
regret to say a large portion of the Cuban ladies
have a very limited education, and especially are
they said to be deficient in <u>writing</u>, perhaps this
is wisely forbidden by <u>los viejos</u> (the old folks),
consequently their amatory epistles are very few
and far between. I have from a seat on the <u>Alameda
d'Paula</u>, watched some of these outdoor court-
ships with a good deal of interest, and been much
amused by the skill the young lady exhibits to
prevent discovery.

I should judge that but few people in Havana
pay much attention to religious services on the
sabbath. The churches are opened at a very early
hour, and the service is ended before twelve o'clk,
and they are not crowded except at the celebra-
tion of some extra ordinary Mass, or especially
good music to be enjoyed. I should judge that the
whole Sunday service is completed during the fifteen or twenty minutes that Mass lasts, and the
rest of the day devoted to parties, excursions, din-

ners, and all kinds of amusements. The theaters
are more crowded on that evening than any other
of the week. The artillery band (the favorite one
with the Captain General) plays this evening, (the
same as any other,) on the <u>Plaza d' Armas</u> and
another on the <u>Paseo Facon</u>, which is crowded
with volantes, promenaders and horsemen, while
the soldiers make an unusual display on this day,
by sham fights, etc., and bullfights <u>always</u> come
off on Sundays. I am of opinion that the Cubanos
are not very devoted partizans of the Pope, as they
say, they neither believe in the infallibility of the
Roman pontiff, nor buy any <u>bulls</u> except that
termed of <u>the dead</u>, without which no consecrated
grave is allowed to any person. The boxes
(<u>confessionarios</u>) in the churches provided for con-
fession are generally empty, and I have noticed,
where there is more than one priest in church, except the one officiating, they go to sleep in their
comfortable chairs, and when their services are
required a little bellboy arouses them. The young
men, while in church, talk and laugh all the time
and criticize the ceremonies. Nearly all of the
stores are kept open on Sunday and it is in fact a
general holiday.

The ceremonies attendant upon a funeral here
are worthy of note, as soon as a person dies, his
will is produced, which generally states the
manner in which the burial shall take place, and
the amount of the several legacies which every
testator is <u>compelled</u> by royal orders to bequeath
and the number of Masses required to be celebrated in favor of his soul. Another thing is indispensable to buy the <u>bull for the dead</u>, which

costs quarter of an ounce (four and one-quarter dollars). This is in fact paying a tax to government for the privilege of going out of the world. Licenses are required from the priest in order that the corpse may be admitted to the cemetery, and from the guards stationed at the city gate, who will not permit the hearse to pass without it. A kind of <u>wake</u> is kept up for about twenty-four hours after death, the corpse being exposed to view, dressed in its richest clothing, and sometimes being elevated on a board, so as to be seen at the window by passersby. The undertaker furnishes mourners, and the immediate family and friends do not accompany the dead to their final resting place. Before arriving at the burial ground (<u>campo santo</u>) the coffin is taken from the hearse at the Beneficencia asylum, and carried to the chapel, where the mendicant girls sing a chant, etc., which costs an ounce ($17) and affords a good income to the institution. Another responsary is sung at the cemetery, where there is a small chapel. During the prayers the coffin is lowered into the grave and quickly covered, previously being thickly overlaid with quicklime. No monument or stones are seen, except occasionally a flat slab lying horizontally on the ground covering the grave. The burial grounds are most disgusting spectacles, being full of bones and parts of decayed bodies, for but very few graves remain untouched more than three months, and it is considered by that time the body has gone to dust again (or ought to), and the ground is dug over again for another occupant. The last resting place is anything <u>but</u> hallowed ground.

TODAY I NOTICE fresh blossoms on the orange trees, while the boughs hang heavy with the fruit of last year, which will hold out until the new fruit is ripe in August, so <u>fresh</u> oranges can be picked through the year. Bananas, plantains, coconuts, and pineapples, and other fruits, are budding and ripening at the same time, throughout the year, for it is <u>always summer</u> here.

I have just been out in the <u>portreros</u>, picking and eating <u>guavas</u>. This delightful fruit grows wild, and from it is made the rich guava jelly and marmalade which is sold in small boxes in the States. It is about as common here on the table as apple or any ordinary fruit sauce at home. The tree (about the size of our peach) grows without any cultivation, and is found all over the island. The putting up of these <u>dulces</u> or sweetmeats for exportation is quite a business in Havana and Cardenas.

I ought to make an apology (even to myself), for the rambling style of my journal and letters to the *Times* newspaper but they are written, just as I am in the vein, without any forethought or preparation, and I give my impressions of Cuba, just as I receive them, many probably crude and perhaps incorrect, as to statistics, etc., but what I have seen I give <u>as</u> I have seen with Yankee eyes. I presume there are many repetitions in the journal and letters as I do not read it over after once writing it but it may probably be digested as well as the Spanish do a dish of all sorts, composed of all kinds of vegetables, fish, flesh, and fowl, with quantum sufficit of olive oil, garlics and red pepper, which when finished is called "olla podrida" which is being interpreted a dish of all kinds.

Thursday, March 3

A DESCRIPTION of the birds which are common here would fill books. There are some with most brilliant plumage, comprising the most gorgeous of colors, and the song of others is sweet beyond all description. I have seen several birds which we are familiar with at the North, among them the barn swallow, the rice bird or bobolink, the Baltimore oriole, summer yellow bird, yellow-winged sparrow, cuckoo, heron and sandpiper, also the mockingbird, several varieties of hummingbirds and a species of blackbird called the "Jewbird" with a curious looking face and bill, reminding one strongly of a "Jewface." There are a great variety of duck and plover, the names and varieties of which I am ignorant but I have seen the same in New England and the Western States. There is one bird which attracted my attention from the first and is a peculiar feature of the tropics. It is the carrion crow or turkey buzzard, a bird of hideous aspect and evil augury, and like the angel of death wherever he flaps his heavy wings a lifeless body is not far from him. The negroes hold these birds in superstitious dread, for they fancy that the vapors of mortality which attract these birds are emitted from the dying as well as from the dead. Certain it is that their sense of smell is very acute, for even a few minutes after any dead animal is exposed, the air is black with these foul birds. The turkey buzzard has a striking resemblance to a turkey, being the same shape, but smaller in size and in color a sooty black; around his beak hangs a loose red skin and this together with its bald head, give it a disgusting appearance. Ugly as they are, no one ever disturbs them, for they do the work of scavengers, and perform their filthy business with wonderful celerity. Tenth letter to *Times* today.

Friday, March 4

THERE ARE three or four plagues or torments in this country that never cease their depredations and annoyances. I mean mosquitoes and fleas, ants and cockroaches. The latter eat your boots, clothes, buttons, and toenails; the ants your provisions, and one species, your house, and all kinds of vegetation, while the mosquitoes and fleas, more modest, eat nothing but yourself, especially if you are a newcomer. In proportion to its size the mosquito is certainly one of the most venomous of creatures, and were it the size of a cockroach and its venom in proportion to such a magnitude, I think its bite would certainly produce death. Small as it is, the bite produces any quantity of irritation both of the cellular tissues and nervous system. One of the most extraordinary insects here is the <u>cocuyos</u> or firefly. Myriads of these insects hover at night over the cane fields, and illuminate the hedges with sparkles of phosphoric fire. The smallest are about the size of our common housefly and some larger than bumblebees, and the light they produce is strong enough to light a dark room tolerably well. When the insect is irritated its phosphorescence is so strong that in the dark I have been able to read a letter by holding the fly over the lines and moving it along. In the rainy season their numbers greatly increase, and they are sometimes taken in quantities and put into vials and paper cages to illuminate a room, which they do very prettily. They can be kept for a long time by being bathed daily in water and fed on sugarcane.

A little animal called the lizard, of the chameleon species, is very common here, running about the door yard, shrubs, and house. It has the power of changing its color and putting on the hue of every twig or flower on which it rests. It is an unoffensive little thing, and appears somewhat fond of the society of man, as they are easily tamed so as to be fed from the hand. A few snakes are found here, but they are perfectly harmless, none being poisonous. The scorpion which is occasionally seen is the only reptile whose bite is considered at all dangerous, excepting the hairy black spider, whose bite is poisonous, and sometimes said to be fatal, and this and the scorpion are, to say the least, so unpleasant as to be particularly

avoided. The monster spider is a horrible looking
reptile some two or three inches in length, but it
is said to be quite as harmless as ours of the
"daddy longleg" species. I think from what I have
seen and heard there are less <u>venomous</u> insects
and reptiles here than we find in the North. I had
no intention of writing a chapter on natural history when I commenced, and as I make no pretensions to being a naturalist, I think I will "dry
up" on the subject. Wrote several letters home this
evening.

Saturday, March 5

I N THE COUNTRY here no one rides abroad without
being armed. Every horseman we meet carries
sword and pistols, and even the negroes carry
knives and <u>machetes</u>. The arming of the guarijos
or yeomanry has always been encouraged by the
authorities (though a law of the land prohibits the
carrying of deadly weapons) for they thus form a
sort of mounted militia, at all times an available
and effective arm against negro insurrection. The
<u>guajiros</u> are not generally slave owners, <u>but</u> em-
ployed as overseers make the hardest of task masters as they seem to have a natural antipathy to
the blacks. The bugbear which is often raised, of
the freeing of the slaves by the government in case
of an invasion, amounts to just nothing, as half a
dozen of these white men, united and determined
and withal well armed are more than a match for
fifty ignorant and superstitious blacks.

Sunday, March 6

BUSY WRITING letters to home, etc., this morning and finished eleventh letter for the *Times*. Riding over to the tavern this morning we were reminded that the <u>carnival</u> commenced last evening, and that there were to be balls every evening, and a cockfight this afternoon at Hato Nuevo. As we were intending to start for Cardenas early in the morning we anticipated by going as far as Hato Nuevo this afternoon. We took the volante, and had Domingo follow with our saddle horses. We arrived just in the midst of the entertainment at the cockpit. This was a temporary building of stakes, with a low palm-leaf roof, and of all the spectacles I ever witnessed this was one of the most amusing. The excitability of the Spanish and Creole population was here fully brought out, and money was freely bet on the birds and freely changed hands. The gestures, shouts and badinage in which all participated, both old and young, made the cockpit a perfect pandemonium. This sport was indulged in by men of gray hairs, women who might have appeared to better advantage elsewhere, and children of tender years and all without regard to color, for here niggers, and white[s] all seemed about equal, and nearly all were smoking, under this little low roof, and all presided over by no less a personage than our friend the <u>Captain d' Partido</u>, or captain of this partido or district. A partido consists of a number of towns or villages, this one composing an area of some fifteen or twenty miles each way, and the capitan is military commandant, civil judge and police magistrate for these limits. The office is generally bestowed upon some retired army officer (for it is customary if not obligatory upon all officers getting married to retire from active military service, unless specially permitted to retain their position).

We made the acquaintance of Don José Bonanz, "Captain of the Robber Catcher" as he is called, who is stationed here with some dozen soldiers or so to protect this section of the country from robbers. We found him an intelligent and gentlemanly man and who has acquaintances in New York, known to me although he has never visited the States. He is trying to learn English and I Spanish so we had a comfortable time. He plays on the flute very well and I whistled "Yankee Doodle" to him until he caught the air and plays it very well. We dined at the capitan's and in the evening visited a country ball where the capitan's sister, Señorita Elenor, was the belle. (A good sized belle too for she must have weighed 180 pounds.) Don José introduced me to several of the ladies, but I notice only their christened name was mentioned as Señoritas Pastora, Satharia, Antoinetta, Carolina, Catalina, etc., etc. The only dance was the Spanish contra danza, which is mostly a waltz, and I notice that one dance occupied about an hour, being only a repetition of the same figure until the dancers were well fatigued. I did not participate. I saw here the big spiders crawl up through the large holes in the floor, some of which I should judge were six inches in circumference. Captain Bonanz was especially agreeable and urged us to stay and see the end of the ball, but I was too tired. The dresses of the ladies would hardly pass at the North, as those who evidently considered themselves the best dressed wore every variety of color and their headdresses were a perfect curiosity as to shape, style, and colors. We started between twelve o'clk to ride to the St. Catalina distant some three leagues, accompanied by <u>Domingo</u>. We gallop off in the pitch of darkness, our sure-footed ponies keeping the road without nay trouble. We have the usual night accompaniment of travellers here, for every time we pass a house or hovel we arouse the dogs and have them barking at our heels for half a mile, though we stilled several by shots from my little revolver. The night air was cool and damp and almost oppressive with the rich odor of the night blooming jasmine, the oleander, the orange blossom, and the many flowers which line the roads and savannahs which we pass. A few rods of the hedges here would furnish shrubs and flowers to fill a northern hothouse, whose sickly inmates would shrink from a comparison with the gay prodigals of field and fence which lavish their sweetness here on the public highway. Columbus felt and appreciated all these beauties, when he wrote to King Ferdinand, saying—"I had almost come to the resolution of staying here the remainder of my days; for believe me, sirs, these lands far surpass all the rest of the world in pleasure and convenience."

The ashes of the great discoverer now repose in the old cathedral in Havana in the beautiful island where [he] expressed his desire of remaining. We arrive at Bittun's, and get on our cots about two o'clk and <u>try</u> to sleep, but the mosquitoes <u>buz</u> and <u>bite</u>, and the <u>fleas</u> (I have brought away from the ball) <u>jump</u> and <u>bite</u>, so that quiet is impossible and after tossing about for three hours we get up, and take oranges and coffee, and mount our horses and start for <u>Recreo</u> station.

Monday, March 7

A T THE RECREO, I saw the <u>skate</u> advertisement posted up on the depot and a crowd who could not either read or understand looking at it. It has been there for a fortnight past and no one dares to take it down. We took the train after waiting a couple of hours, to put a car on the track and got into Cardenas by ten o'clk. It being carnival time no business could be transacted. We took a saltwater bath in the bathing house off the end of the long wharf, and soaked ourselves long enough in saltwater to counteract the effect of the fleas and mosquitoes and amused ourselves by taking and drowning the first named of these insects. I have been a perfect martyr and can count my wounds by the scores.

For three days all Cuba has been at play, and tomorrow (March 8) is the last day of the carnival, finishing the commencement of Ash Wednesday. It has been celebrated by bullfights, cockfights, military parades, ringing of bells, balls, masquerades, tournaments, etc., etc. At Cardenas here the holiday is general, all business suspended even the banks being closed. The ladies hold a grand fair or <u>bazaar</u> at the new market house, and have (as I can testify) manifested as much skill in disposing of tickets in worthless lotteries, as ever our Hartford ladies do in charitable and church fairs. One thing was slightly different—gambling was carried on openly in the rotunda, and tables where the poor darkey lost his <u>real</u>, were side by side, with those where the rich won and lost their piles of ounces. I counted <u>twenty-two</u> different kinds of games, from the <u>sweat cloth</u>, we used to see at general trainings to the <u>monte</u> bank where hundreds are staked. The Spaniards are inveterate gamblers, and it was told with a magnificent air that a certain marquis had come to Cardenas with sixty-eight thousand dollars in gold to bet on cocks, monte, etc., and another had credit of twenty-three thousand dollars at bank for the same purpose. I saw sixpences and ounces lost just the same, without a show of regret or a change of countenance. Occasionally some one would win a handful of ounces, but generally the bankers <u>skinned</u> the victims of all they had. In the evening there was to be a grand masquerade ball, attended by all the aristocracy of Cardenas and vicinity; at the door all females were required to unmask to prevent the entrance of those of known bad character, and all men to show their bare hands to prevent negroes from being admitted. At the cockfight yesterday an American present and betting, was asked his name and he gave it as <u>Buchanan</u>. The Spaniards crowded around and stared at him as if he was a wild animal and some asked if he had really come to buy the island. Many said is it the <u>President</u> Buchanan, but were satisfied when told, no, that it was his <u>brother-in-law</u>! The thirty million bill is still the great topic of discussion at every corner and the filibusters are not few nor far between here. Crittenden's and Thompson's speeches in the U.S. Senate are commented on and criticized in terms not very complimentary. All kinds of rumors prevail, one day the bill has passed and the Spanish minister demanded his passports and left Washington—next day, that the bill is defeated in the Senate and will be in the House. One creole gentleman says to me, "if the bill is defeated now, we hope still, but it is hard to look forward to another year of misery." We could not stay in Cardenas overnight among the "congrejos" (crabs) and mosquitoes and as Ned Wilson was not in town we took the three o'clk P.M. train for Recreo.

The railroads in this country are badly managed, and the cars are generally old and engines defective, for want of proper shops and capable workmen to repair them. The track is imperfectly laid, and when running off the track as trains frequently do, it is without any proper tools, a work of time to put matters to rights. The roads are principally used for the transportation of sugar and molasses, and the cars, track, depots, etc., are coated with saccharine matter, and I notice the engineer carries a pan of wood ashes to sprinkle upon the track, as the locomotive driving wheels slip on the molasses etc. The average rate of speed is twelve miles an hour, and this is on a perfectly level savanna make[s] accidents very rare, but with the dust and cigar smoke (for everybody smokes in the cars), makes railroad traveling rather inconvenient, to say the least and for ladies

somewhat impleasant. I notice a marked difference where there are Spanish and American engineers. The engines run by the former, are filthy
and dirty to the last degree, but if there is a piece
of brass in a conspicuous place, it is polished
brightly, but the iron and steel work is covered
with rust, dirt, and grease. The oil used is the sweet
or olive oil, which is brought from Spain (of course
duty free) and is sold here at about eighty cents
[a] gallon. The railroads were formerly owned by
government, but are now mostly in the hands of
private companies.

Tuesday, March 8

WE STOPPED at Recreo only a few minutes and
took horses directly for Hato Nuevo, where
there was to be another ball, last night being the
last one of the carnival. We rode sharp and arrived
just at dusk—We took dinner at a Spanish tavern
and had bull beef, smoked fish and a bottle of olives. We managed to secure a good bottle of cham-
pagne and some good coffee, but felt like shutting
my eyes to the look of things. So much filth near
and around my feeding place I never saw before.
It beat [. . .] and out West completely. The table
cloth which is only laid in these taverns for gentlemen (so the landlord said) was a nondescript color.
Age, dirt, and Catalan wine made it hardly
distinguishingable from the dark cedar table.
There was an apology for a <u>castor</u> on the table but
of such antiquated pattern that I declared it to be
the one Columbus had used coming over and on

referring to the landlord he said he presumed it was, but did not exactly know, but certainly just as the <u>caballeros</u> chose about it. It reminded me of the cockney showman who when asked by his children spectators, which was the elephant, and which the monkey replied—"whichever you pleases my little dears, you've paid your money and you takes your choice." I <u>staid round</u> the ball until eleven o'clk and finding John to be determined to stay longer and dance, I took <u>Domingo</u> and started for San Ricardo alone, (or rather alone with a negro following). The ball was a repetition of the previous night with the same belles and same music. As I rode toward home the music of the old drum and piccolo with occasionally the toot of the horn floated over the night air, accompanied by the negro melodies from the sugarhouse at <u>Teneria</u>. The night was dark but I trusted friend Domingo's horse "<u>Polidore</u>" who was sure footed and with a loose rein I rode at full speed over the road, and arrived safe about twelve o'clk. The dogs were wide awake and received me with a chorus of barking, but as I have become friends with all (except old Panetela) I dismount, and am soon in bed and sleep so sound I did not know when John came in two hours after. In speaking of the carnival amusements and the various games, etc., I omitted to speak of one, peculiar and worthy of note, but an amusement so cruel as to be disgusting. It is however an old <u>Spanish</u> custom and that accounts for its cruelty. It is called the <u>corrida de patos</u> or duck race. An old and tough duck is hung from a strong branch of a tree with its head downward at such a height that a man on horseback and riding at full speed may catch hold of the neck, and pull the head off. To make the feat more difficult, the neck is covered with grease which causes the hand to slip, and the sufferings of the poor bird are prolonged. A crowd of mounted guajiros are stationed at a given point, from which they start successively and try their strength on the bird. The victory was finally won by a strong armed fellow who was presented with a sash of gay colored ribbon by the queen of the festival. All the inhabitants of Hato Nuevo and other residents of the neighborhood were present and also the Capitan de Partido who authorized this innocent and intellectual amusement.

Wednesday, March 9

JOHN AND MYSELF started at noon to go up to see Joe Wilson on the estate of Nueva Esperanza (New Hope) at Sierra Morena. It is between thirty and forty miles from San Ricardo, and through some beautiful country after crossing the little Rio d' la Palma (River of Palms) we came out on the savannahs and for some eighteen or twenty miles we are crossing this broad gravelly plain covered with the different species of palm some of which are very beautiful. We crossed two or three rapid but (at this season) shallow rivers, whose banks were lined with thick tangled woods and the air rich with the odors of a thousand flowers. The wild mignionette tree as large as our ordinary horse chestnuts at home—the almond tree—the heavy rich-leaved mango tree, the wild oleander, and southern rose and the rich aroma of the vanilla bean, and many rich tropical flowers and trees of which I am ignorant of the names or species. I notice many varieties of convolvulus growing wild over hedges and trees, but of all else the majestic royal palm, sometimes with its trunk smooth and white, rising some ninety feet in height and then its graceful tuft of massy leaves give to the interior of Cuba an aspect which cannot fail to impress a stranger. The graceful coconut tree too with its clusters of rich green fruit, <u>looks</u> tempting enough to charm an anchorite. Each object on this ride, both natural and artificial <u>stand out</u> in the clear liquid light, and there is none of the haze (so peculiar to our own northern climate at certain season) to intercept the view. We pass through <u>Palma Sola</u> and Santa Barbara and other little clusters of houses of which I forget the names and after leaving the savannahs we strike through a range of heavy timbered hills, and where an opening comes, we catch a distant view of old ocean with his blue waters glittering under a tropical sun. While riding through the country, I was struck by the great extent of unimproved land which is evidently susceptible of cultivation. In the hands of an industrious, thrifty and <u>go-ahead</u> population, Cuba would blossom like the rose; now it is a garden growing wild, cultivated here and there in patches, but capable at least of supporting in ease a population of ten times its present number. It is impossible to describe how <u>completely everything</u> differs from what we see in the States. The climate, the people, manners and customs, the foliage, fruit, flowers, vegetables and general products, the architecture, business, labor, and form of government, each and all present such a striking contrast to what a Yankee sees at home, and yet this strange country is only five or six days distant from New York, about twelve hundred miles only. The scenery of the island is decidedly oriental, and reminds one of the many descriptions we have all read of the Eastern world. The style of building and the trees and vegetables must bear a strong resemblance to the Orient. Here—we have, "Larger constellations burning, mellow moons and happy skies, Breadths of tropic shade and palms in cluster, knots of Paradise," and, "Droops the heavy blossom'd tower, hangs the heavy fruited tree—Summer isle of Eden lying in dark purple spheres of sea." Tennyson must have lived in the tropics or he could never have written these words.

Thursday, March 10

JOE WAS very glad to see us last evening and gave us a capital dinner and plenty of <u>bueno vino</u> to wash it down. We talked, played chess, etc., until late and went to bed and slept sound after our long ride. The house here is built more like our New England houses. Two stories high and a basement and got up in some style, wooden floors, glass windows etc. The land in this vicinity is lower, and at certain seasons liable to be almost overflowed, and for that cause is built after this style. There is a large broad veranda in front, and here we sit and read and talk and smoke all day long. Of course we have visited the sugar mill, purging house, and all the various buildings attached to the place. This estate is owned by the D'Wolf family of Bristol (Frank D. W.) and Wilson is administrator. It is [a] much larger estate than San Ricardo, and employs about 350 negroes and produces nearly 4000 boxes of sugar, or will this year. And from where we sit on the piazza I can see the coconut tree loaded with its delicious fruit, the tamarind tree covered with those little pods containing its agreeable acid, and the delicious orange waiting to be plucked and eaten. Close by the houses is a large salbiedeira or sandbox tree with its curious fruit which when peeled makes a perfect sandbox. We have been luxuriating in coconut milk or water I should call it clear, cool and refreshing. I find it particularly good about mid-day and contrive to dispose of several large tumblers full. We tasted of the pulp which is soft and can be eaten with a spoon but the liquid is far preferable. Tamarind water and drink made from a fruit called soursop are very generally used as a beverage here. Although wine is always placed before strangers, and the Catalan or red wine upon the table and used freely by all at the table, yet since I have been in Cuba, I have only seen one man intoxicated, and he was not very drunk, but merry and somewhat excited at the cockfight a few days ago. I believe such is the case in all wine farming and wine consuming countries. Grapes will not grow on the island and all the wine is brought from Spain and France duty free, and sells at much less prices than with us at the North, and as I am induced to believe to be a much purer and better article.

The Catalan or red wine so common here, sells by the pipe, and is priced at $40 to $60 a pipe according to the quality—averaging say forty-five cents a gallon.

Friday, March 11

I T IS SAID to be an old Spanish proverb, that "<u>fruit is gold in the morning, silver at noon and lead at night</u>." Undoubtedly there is figurative truth in this aphorism, but the fruit here <u>tastes</u> good at all times and all hours, but more especially just after getting out of bed in the early morning. Oranges are scarce here just now, as they have all been picked, the orchard being young and small, but they have here a species of plum (the name I have forgotten) which is as big as my fist, weighs perhaps from half to three-quarters of a pound and is of a most delicious flavor. Have been writing several letters home today, but as the mosquitoes and sand flies are so thick here it is hard work— write with one hand and brush away the tormenting little devils with the other. We intended to ride down to San Ricardo this evening but as the moon is obscured by cloud[s] etc., we have concluded to start just before daybreak. We played chess this evening and <u>lotteria,</u> a game of chance, and Jo and

myself won all of John's odd shillings, though John
said we cheated—We retired about 11:30 P.M.

Saturday, March 12

W E WERE UP at 3:00 A.M. but I did not feel well
and did not start until about 4:00 A.M. We
had light enough from the planet Venus which
appears very much larger and brighter than at the
North. We took a different route from the one we
came and passed some beautiful spots on the road.
The usual perfume of flowers, made the air heave
with their odors. About half way my horse lamed
and his gait was very uncomfortable, so we
pushed out of our road some five or six miles toward an acquaintance of John's named Lawton
who has an estate called Santa Rosa. Here we proposed to leave the lame horse for a day or two
and take a fresh one, without delay, but Sr. Lawton
insisted on our staying to breakfast, and politeness compelled us to do so tho' we were poorly
paid for the delay, for the table was filthy and all
the white men on the place fed together and acted
like hogs at the table—Lawton is a burly English-
man who doesn't pinch his stomach, but he has
no authority and commands no respect. His sugar
making is on an improved plan with vacuum pans
and clarifying, etc., and he turns out a quality of
fine sugar as white as snow itself. With a horse
belonging to his mayoral we started for home distant some eighteen miles and made it in two hours.

Being somewhat fatigued after so long a ride in the middle of the day, I took a <u>siesta</u>, which I have found to be a kind of institution here and by dinner time, 4:30 P.M., I feel as good as new.

I notice the inhabitants here are badly given to lying, and I find <u>perjury</u> in this country is not considered a criminal offence, because it is so common that but few having legal business to transact swear to anything but to what is their own benefit without any regard to the truth. The fatal fault of all Spanish-Americans, Mexicans, etc., is their want of truthfulness. It is their fatal facility for making oaths and breaking them—for setting up governments and conspiring against them—which had been their own ruin and that of their country. They inherited this quality from their forefathers and each subsequent generation has improved upon it.

Of the personal habits of the Spaniards I have spoken before, and it is proved by the testimony of many Spanish writers that cleanliness has not been inherited from their ancestors. A certain friar, <u>Gerundio</u>, published a work not many years since and says the following incident actually happened to himself: on arriving at a country in a town in Spain, and not finding water to wash his hands and face, covered with perspiration and dust after his journey, he called for some. On the following morning he felt unwell as he had taken a slight fever, which confined him to his room for a week, at the expiration of which time he concluded to leave and again called for water to wash with. "How is that?" responded the hostess, "Did you not wash yourself the day you arrived?" Many

Spaniards I have met <u>may</u> have washed themselves on their <u>arrival</u> from Spain, some time since,
but appearances certainly indicate they haven't
washed <u>since</u>.

A coffee estate or plantation is a garden of
beauty and is a characteristic of this climate, which
must be seen to be appreciated. Having only seen
one from a distance. I speak as much from what I
have learned from others, as from my own observation. The land is planted in regular squares of
several acres in extent, each, and intersected by
broad avenues of orange, palm, coconut, caimito
and other ornamental and fruits trees of the tropics. The coffee plant requires to be protected partially from the sun, and for this cause shade trees,
are planted in their midst. Among these trees and
along the walks, are planted bananas, lemons,
pomgranites, oleanders, cape jasmines, roses, and
heliotropes filling the air with fragrance. The coffee blossom is white as snow and so abundant that
it seems as if the plants were covered with them.
Fruit trees are scattered abundantly all over an
estate, and it is a perfect flower garden with almost every luxury the heart could wish for. The
coffee plant is much less cultivated than formerly
on the island, as sugar yields a much better in-
vestment on capital. The cause of this is the decline in the price of coffee, owing to the increased
importation from the East Indies, Arabia, and
South America. The coffee grown on the island is
the most delicious I ever tasted and brings by the
quantity some eighteen cents per pound. I presume none of it goes to the United States owing
to this large price and duties on it.

It is evident that the soil of Cuba is peculiarly adapted to the raising of sugar and tobacco, and although almost everything vegetable may be grown here, these two staples must continue to be the great produce of the island. The extensive savannahs extending in some cases over fifty miles in length, are now used only for <u>porteros</u> or pastures, but it is said <u>cotton</u> can be profitably raised on these neglected lands. I have some samples of the green seed cotton grown here without cultivation, which in appearance is equal to the far famed <u>sea island</u> cotton. The wild cotton grows here in great profusion, and if cultivated would probably be equal to the staple cotton of our southern states.

The cultivation of tobacco here is not as profitable as many suppose and a great portion raised is vastly inferior to that grown in our own Connecticut valley. Its cultivation is costly, requiring a new soil of great fertility and a great amount of heat. The tobacco growers do not manure their lands, and I doubt if there is used on the island any kind of artificial manures. When land becomes worn here, it is abandoned and new lands taken for there is a perfect wilderness of wild and uncultivated lands particularly on the eastern section of the island.

The choicest tobacco grown here is from the <u>Vuelto d' Abajo</u>, a section situated in the western part of the island. The growers in this section are very skillful but not scientific, and generally forward their tobacco to Havana, for speculators who advance the price, before the cutting. When the crops come in they go out to witness the making

up of the bales in order to prevent their being sold
to others, or changed for an article of inferior quality, to prevent which great care is necessary.

The consumption of cigars is enormous on the
island. It <u>seems</u> as if every man, woman, and child
smoked and it is not an uncommon thing to see a
lady smoking a cigarette in her own parlor, for
the floors are almost on the level with the street.
(The doors and windows are all open, and at a
glance the eye penetrates the whole interior of
domestic life, from the flowers in the court yard
to the daughter's bed with its white muslin cur-
tains tied with red and blue ribbons.) The men of
all degrees smoke, and smoke everywhere: in the
streets, in the houses, in cafes, theatres, counting
rooms and while eating and drinking. The shoe-
maker over his lapstone and the tailor over his
goose, all smoke, smoke and the first courtesy offered you by a Cuban is the everlasting cigar.
Many gentlemen consume from ten to twenty
(<u>large</u> and <u>long</u> and <u>strong</u>) cigars a day while
others are almost always with a cigaritto between
their lips. The result of this large and increasing
consumption including the heavy export of the
article is to employ an immense number of
persons in the manufacture of cigars, and little
stalls and stores are to be found all over the city,
at every corner. And through all the principal
streets where cigars and cigarittos are made and
sold.

Snuff takers are rarely seen and so far I have
met but with very few persons who <u>eat</u> or chew
tobacco and those were mostly Yankees who are
domesticated here.

Sunday, March 13

THIS MORNING the <u>correo</u> (postman) brought me several letters from home and files of New York papers, etc. I finished several letters myself from home and fourteenth letter for the *Times*. Tomorrow noon Captain Bonanz, Señorita Ellenor and the wife of the Captain of Partido with niggers and children came up to dine and spend the day. We exerted ourselves to please and passed the day very agreeably. The principal feature was dinner which was fully discussed by all hands. The savannahs north of the house took fire this afternoon and for a little time all was confusion. Don Ricardo had gone to Cardenas, so John was off, and with our Ricardo, negroes, and a gang from Teneria, the fire was fought back, and no serious damage done though the distillery came near going. Great care is exercised to prevent fires for if a cane field takes fire, it spreads with great rapidity and a short time would suffice to burn an entire estate and the loss would be very heavy. Especially at this dry season must great care be exercised, for a fire once started it is almost impossible to check it except by fighting it back with fire—burning toward the fire the same way as our western people do the high grass on the prairies.

The colored population of the island is estimated at about eight hundred thousand, in which estimate the free negroes are included, amounting to an insignificant proportion. The free negroes in the town are journeymen laborers; many are artisans, few have shops and fewer still are the proprietors of small houses. It is not uncommon for them to know how to read, and even write; but they generally attain only a very limited knowledge of these important requisites. The majority of negroes are addicted to vice and but few evince a virtuous disposition. A very few amass even a moderate competence as they commonly waste their earnings and first earnings, and no considerable amount of money ever falls into their hands, unless they draw a prize in the Havana lottery, in which nearly all buy tickets. Their wants are few, and they consider themselves happy if they can barely subsist, drink <u>aquadiente</u>, [<u>aguardiente</u>] smoke and dance on Sundays and feast days. The native or creole negroes are less economical than those brought from Africa, who are generally very avaricious, and sometimes die from want of nourishment by the side of their <u>botigas</u>, or jars full of money. Free negroes and mulattoes in the country are generally just the contrary of those of the same class in town for they are hard working, honorable, and honest—some take farms on a lease, which they cultivate with care and good judgment; and though a wealthy negro is seldom seen in the country, yet many live in comparative comfort, despite the exactions they receive from officials, who plunder them to the utmost extent by pretexts and infamous exactions. The slaves in Cuba have certain rights, of which they are deprived in the United States. One of the authorities called the <u>sindico</u>, sees that these rights are fully enjoyed, and he cannot exact anything from the negroes, though they may possess property. He can compel the owner of the negro to give him permission for three days absence to look for another master without being obliged to assign the cause. If the owner values his negro at too high a price, appraisers are appointed to regulate it. The slave can also at any time give money to his master on account of the price of his freedom and require him to declare what that price is, and it cannot be raised afterwards for any cause. Those who have given fifty dollars or over are called coartados, and they are entitled to have certain days to themselves, and are sometimes allowed to work on their own account by paying to the master one real daily for each hundred dollars of the price. It is by no means uncommon to meet with slaves, who having [the] requisite amount of money do not want to obtain liberty, and this too, on sugar plantations where the work is the hardest. Many of the negroes (particularly it is the case with native Africans) have the singular pleasure of keeping all their earnings in earthen pots buried in the ground and they sometimes die carrying the secret with them. A parcel of land is allotted to each negro every year, the products of which belong to him, and it is devoted to the cultivation of yuca, rice, okra, peanuts, sweet potatoes, corn, etc., etc., during his leisure hours. Besides Sundays there are many days throughout the year, when by laws of Church and State, all work is suspended. Slaves are allowed to raise a pig, poultry, and sometimes a mare, and they can always find a market for their stock at the nearest tavern, or sell to their masters. Many have accumulated sufficient money to buy their wives and children and themselves, and it is a fact, that a negro owner is the worst of tyrants to his slave. When work is pressing, a bargain is sometimes made with the slaves to labor on feast days at about fifty cents a day. This price is allowed them also for a cord of wood cut during their own time. They are supplied daily with plenty of food consisting of <u>tasajo</u> or jerked beef, dried fish, plantain, rice, and various vegetables growing here. The two principal dishes for the negro are <u>funché</u>, or hominy, and plantains, and these they prefer to all others. Two or three times a year (<u>always</u> on Christmas), a shirt and pantaloons are given to each male, and a gown to the female, and occasionally a fancy cotton handkerchief for a head dress too, but a blanket and woolen jacket which is given Christmas is the event of the whole year. All negroes desire to have a thick pilot-cloth short jacket such as sailors wear and are quite as likely to put it on while the thermometer stands at 90°—as during a norther and the mercury at 60°. Clothing here is one of the least of the wants of the negro, for they would in most cases go entirely naked if allowed to do so.

Cuba has been called the hot-bed of slavery, and it is in a certain sense true, but I claim as a general thing, the slaves have more privileges than in the States. The slave trade still flourishes (and if reports may be believed it does also in the United States in 1859!) though a much less number are imported than in former years. The effect of this is to raise the price of slaves and procure for them better treatment. An able bodied male slave is now valued at an average of $1200 to $1500, and some good house servants are held at over $2,000. A slave when first landed, is worth if sound from three to five hundred dollars, and as he becomes more acclimated and instructed, for their dull natures require a vast deal of training before they can be brought to any position of usefulness, in doing which the overseers have found kindness to go much farther than harshness. Trifling rewards, for services soon establish a good understanding, and they soon grow very tractable though it is a long time before they understand a word of Spanish. The various African tribes are so strongly marked that there is no difficulty in knowing their nationality. The Congoes and those from the Gold Coast are the most numerous. The former are small, but quick and make good laborers. The Santees, Ashantees, and Carrobalees are larger races, more uneasy and powerful at home, and are more rarely conquered in battle or taken prisoner by the shore tribes in Africa, who sell them to slave factories on the coast. There is a mulatto tribe called Ebroes who make excellent domestic servants. The negroes fresh from Africa called <u>bozales,</u> are almost pitiful to look upon, and one cannot but feel that however hard their future life may be, it cannot but be an improvement upon their previous life. They are the most filthy, ignorant and degraded of the human species. In fact they are animal in their natures and nothing else, and it seems almost an impossibility that such beings should possess a mind. There is one class known as dirt-eaters, who will if allowed, eat the soil of the island in such quantities as to produce death. These are supposed to be cannibals or man-eaters; and the resident slaves always keep their children away from newly imported slaves. One nigger mother told me, they would eat her picanininies if they could catch them. Of clothing and its uses they have no conception, and as for any feeling of humanity towards each other, they have none at all, for they sometimes die for want of nourishment or medicine, while sick, and the one near them, would not raise his hand to help his dying fellow creature, but will steal his blanket, or anything he has on, before the breath has left his body.

Sometimes an epidemic gets among the slaves and sweeps them off by hundreds. There are many reasons for this—their carelessness and imprudence in eating and drinking, their extreme filth, and above all, the fact that medicine sometimes seems to have no visible effect. It takes more than twice as much medicine to affect a negro as it does [a] white man here, but the reason is a mystery to me. The prevailing sickness among the negroes is diseases of the bowels, and for this reason their food is regularly rationed out to them, but they eat fruit immoderately where it grows in such profusion, and the consequence is, there are always more or less in the hospital.

The slave trade will exist just so long as Spain holds the island, and it is far from suppressed for only last week Lawton told me of a cargo of over 900 lately landed at St. Juan de los Remedos (near Lavalette's place), and that a cargo is daily expected off his place, which is hardly fifty miles from Cardenas. The government officials and Capitan de Partido are undoubtedly liberally fee'd and no difficulty is experienced in landing on the coast. After getting clear of the English and

American squadrons on the coast of Africa, it is plain sailing and no obstacles. This too, in the face of the treaty obligations which Spain has with other nations. Our American squadron would do more to suppress the slave trade, and also to protect American interests here, if stationed <u>around the island of Cuba</u>, and the time will come I imagine when such will be the case.

The importation of Chinese or coolies, is getting to be quite an important item, and there are a great many of them scattered all over the island. Probably from 60–75,000 and by some have been estimated as high as 300,000. However, less than 50,000 have been entered at Havana and probably of 75,000 will be a larger estimate. The planter pays the importers about $300, and takes the coolie for <u>apprenticeship</u> of eight years, paying him four dollars a month (and his board and clothing same as negroes) for his services. At the end of that term the Chinaman goes back to the celestial country at his own expense, or is obliged to hire himself out for another eight years. Consequently they are in reality slaves earning about $50 a year. They are all fatalists, and have not the least regard for human life, and prefer to sacrifice their life at any time to allowing a finger or joint to be amputated. For any fancied injury or slight the remedy is suicide. They are not as robust as the negroes, and cannot do as much work, and they are of the very lowest class of their countrymen, and their habits are the most vicious, and by amalgamating with the negroes as they necessarily must (as no females are brought over), they introduce a worse system of morals, if possible, than that already tolerated among the blacks. The coolie system is the worst species of slavery and will prove a greater curse to the island than negro slavery. Why do not the abolition <u>philanthropists</u> and the <u>black republicans</u> of our country show sympathy etc., for these unfortunate children of the "flowery land." Is it because their skins are <u>not black</u>?

Monday, March 14

FINISHED UP writing several letters. Been looking around the estate gathering up a few mementos of San Ricardo. Marking name on the old cactus trees in the garden, where <u>Julia</u> and Gertrude marked their names last year. How different everything [is] now! Looking at the carts bringing in cane to the mill today reminded me of the singular way or method which the Cubans have of harnessing or yoking their oxen or bulls, something similar to the custom of Eastern countries. The yoke is placed behind and at the roots of the horns, and fastened to them by the heaviest loads without chafing. The animals always have a hole perforated through their nostrils, through which a rope is passed, rendering them very tractable, and the wildest and most stubborn animals are by this means subdued and can be led anywhere. It is asserted in natural history that the greatest strength of horned animals lies in their head and neck, and here, for once, the Spaniard seems to be ahead of the Yankee, who place the yoke across the neck and breast, and the load is drawn by the impetus of the body as given by the limbs.

Tuesday, March 15

S EVERAL <u>LAST</u> LETTERS for home, etc., today say-ing <u>when</u> they may expect me, as I propose to sail from Havana on the twenty-third. Been pack-ing up and getting my things together to leave here early Thursday morning, intending to stay a few days at Cardenas. Rode down to Hato Nuevo this morning on Don Ricardo's <u>nag</u> and his infernal <u>pace</u> bruised every bone in my body. However, it is my last ride on that horse. Procured my travel-ling license from the Capitan d' Partido and made arrangements for his sister-in-law, Señorita Ellenor, to accompany us to Havana. Seventeenth letter to the *Times* today—An American, with a keen eye to the social and political aspects of life, cannot but appreciate the evils that come under his observation at every step he takes upon this island. One cannot but contrast the political conditions of the Cubans with that of our own country.

The Captain General of Cuba is autocrat of the island, and here almost under our own free flag, exists a government as despotic as that of Russia—and this fact must come under one's own imme-diate observation to be fully realized. The very idea—we pass over a few degrees of latitude, a few days sail from New York, and we seem to step from the present enlightened century back into the dark ages. In this beautiful clime of an eternal summer, we are in a land of political darkness. Closely (within sight from Havana almost) is our own land, where every man is a sovereign, and where taxes are self-imposed, while here the lives, fortunes, and liberty of all are held subject to the will of one individual, with merely a <u>nominal</u> mistress thousands of miles away in another hemisphere. Here each free family pays an average of about five hundred dollars for the support of a bigoted tyranny, yielding an annual revenue of nearly thirty million of dollars, for which they get no equivalent, no representation, and no utterance, for pen and tongue are both prescribed. <u>This</u> is enforced by forty thousand armed hirelings from Spain, and <u>this</u> constitutes "<u>The ever faithful island of Cuba</u>."

With a military force like this in our own country, proportionate to our population we should have a standing army of over a million of bayonets. Cuba lies at present under the armed heel of despotism, and if any one asks, why do <u>they</u> not make an effort for independence? Let him look at these statistics of military force stationed here. The Cubans do not possess the energy and independence of our Northern races, but they are brave and generous, and only need an infusion of our Anglo-Saxon blood to make them stand equal to any nation of the face of God's footstool. No American can stay here any short length of time without having his sympathies aroused; and if the <u>anti-Cuba men</u> would once tread the soil of this island, they would soon become advocates of an early and manifest destiny for the "gem of the Antilles." Let it but became a part and portion of our confederacy and everything will be changed here. A tide of emigration from the States will flow into the island, the wastelands will be reclaimed, and their hidden wealth disclosed; a new system of agricultural economy will be introduced, the woods of the island will furnish material for splendid ships and gorgeous furniture; towns and villages will rise like magic, the whole surface of this garden of the world will burst from bud to a magnificent blossom which will astonish the civilized world.

Wednesday, March 16

LAST DAY at San Ricardo. Busy picking oranges and carefully packing them for home this morning. Packed up sugarcane, grenadilla walking sticks and dulces, besides my own personal baggage intending to get off early tomorrow morning. Eat my quota of oranges fresh from the trees for the last time this morning and took a long ride round the estate. I have become so much attached to San Ricardo that I almost regret to leave it and but for my wife and babies at home I think I would be content to stay here for a long time. The air of the hill country is pure and bracing, and the country life here gives a true idea of the life of a Cuban planter. Such a grove of orange trees as hide the house here I am afraid I shall never again see their equal. Prim round trees about as large as our apple with their golden fruit and bright green leaves sparkling with dew and asking to be eaten. Never have I before experienced <u>complete satisfaction</u> in eating fruit. This evening after dinner John and I play our last game of chess for the present and I go out to the sugarhouse and carpenters shop to say "good buy" to the engineer and carpenter Messrs. Peck and Oaks both good Yankees, from Rhode Island and Maine. We all retire early for we rise before the birds tomorrow.

Thursday, March 17

ABOUT HALF PAST THREE we (Señorita Anita, Don Juan and self) started for Cardenas. I rode in the volante with Anita as far as Hato Nuevo where I took horse and gave up my place to Señorita Ellena. Here we added to our mounted escort by Captain Bonanz and a soldier, a civilian, and negro, so we have now around the volante five mounted caballeros and two negroes besides our calesero (Antonio D'Wolf), so we have but little fear of robbers, besides being prepared to give them a _warm_ reception. Don Ricardo was in a hurry to get us off, fearing we would be too late for cars, but it proved we were two hours and over too early at the Sabinillo depot where we amused ourselves firing at a mark with pistol, etc. Here I found Spanish papers giving a full account of the notorious Sickles affair in Washington.

We finally bid our friends "good bye" and took the cars for Cardenas where we arrived "bag and baggage" at ten o'clk A.M. I found volante and horses waiting for Anita and self to go to Esperanza (Fortun's place). I took horses and followed volante. On the road I was a little startled, by seeing two horsemen stop the volante which was some distance ahead of me. I knew of many robberies on this road within a few days and prepared myself for the worst, so drew out my revolver and spurred forward. On nearing I was greatly surprised to find it to be Fortun and his servant, and after a little chat we pushed on to Esperanza where breakfast was waiting us. I had intended to stay here a few days but find Ed Wilson and Charles and his family have all gone to Matanzas, and the Misses Fales, who we expected to find here, have not arrived and as after tonight, no steamer leaves for Havana until Saturday evening. I have concluded to go on tonight after breakfast. I ride back to Cardenas and John and myself finish up our business affairs and get all our baggage (an army of it too) safely from the depot to the propeller. Rode back to Esperanza with Fortun about five o'clk and dined and then took volante back to Cardenas with Anita. We met Don Juan and onboard our old friend the *Comandantaria* at eight o'clk bound for Havana. The night was beautiful, and a sail along the coast at this season of the year is really delightful. If I ever gazed on enchanting scenery or revelled in the serenity of summer airs, and felt the influence of lovely moonlight, on a placid sea, without a speck on the horizon or a sound on the water except that of the waves caused by our little steamer, as she guided softly and swiftly through the sparkling waters of Cardenas Bay, close along the shore, with the shadows of the blue mountains projecting far beyond us and the white sand beneath clearly visible in the pellucid water as we pass out of the harbor.

The towering peak of the <u>Pan of Matanzas</u> in the distance and the waving trees of palm and coconut on the hills behind the city, give almost the idea of fairyland we read of as children, and imagination easily carries us back to those happy days. No language can give an adequate idea, or convey a thought of the splendid reflection of the moon's beams in every diversity of light and shade on mountain scenery or of that flood of pure etherial lustre which it pours over the fine features of this romantic country. The sea was smooth and on getting outside the harbor our little steamer pushed along bravely, and after a cup of chocolate and a cigar we retired early to our berths.

Friday, March 18

O N WAKING this morning about daybreak found our steamer in her dock in the harbor of Havana just back of Mrs. Almy's hotel. John and myself disposed of our lady passengers with their friends and disposed ourselves and the baggage at the Hotel d' Luz corner Officios and Luz Streets for breakfast. Rademin (the Mayordomo of the house) could not give us rooms or so he said and so we found sleeping accommodations for the present at the <u>Cama d' Catalan</u>, while we took our meals at Madame Almy's. Busy all the morning <u>after</u> a refreshing bath, shampoo, shave, etc. Visited Susiana's great manufactory of cigarittos on <u>Calle d' Cuba</u> and made some pleasant acquaintances. Called to see some of Mr. Rademin's friends who have lived in New York and speak good

English. We drank wine and ate fruit with them, etc., Cuban fashion. I am suffering from a sore throat, etc., today from exposure to night's air last evening in Cardenas. Met several people at Mrs. Almy's lately from the States, and made some very pleasant acquaintances, among others Señor Ortiz, a licenciado (lawyer), from Matanzas, who I met with his wife some years ago in New Haven. Miss Mary McCarr of Richmond, Virginia, who is acquainted with relatives of ours in that city and some gentlemen from New York and Boston—Van Cortland, Simmons etc. Had a row with a soldier today but nothing serious. He insulted our party without cause or provocation but his officer compelled him to apologize. I learn that the total military force now on the island is over forty thousand and this in a population of less than one and a half million. It has been computed that to every four white men on the island there is one soldier. Nearly twenty thousand soldiers are quartered in Havana. To maintain discipline among such a body, the utmost vigor is necessary, and military executions are not infrequent. The garrote is the principal instrument of capital punishment, used here, a machine which chokes the victim to death, without suspending him in the air. The criminal is placed on a chair, leaning his head back upon a support prepared for it, when a ring or collar of iron is drawn up close around the throat. At a given signal a screw is turned from behind which produces instantaneous death, the spinal cord being crushed, where it unites with the brain. Though a repulsive idea, it is certainly more merciful than hanging, where life is destroyed by the slow process of suffocation. The most common mode of execution in the army, however, is the legitimate death of the soldier—to be shot, and when condemned he always falls by the hands of his comrades. The garrote is generally placed just outside the walls, opposite the Cabanas fortress and near the new prison buildings or Punta Fort. It was here the brave Garcia Lopez died a martyr to the cause of Cuban independence. The rear of the barracks close by the Plaza d' Armas, within a few rods of the Captain General's palace, is where the condemned soldiers are made to suffer. The rolling of the drum and the braying of the trumpet are heard in this vicinity at all hours, and the home of the far famed Concha is always guarded by two or three score of soldiers and hundreds more within a few rods at the barracks. This is the man so much respected and beloved by the Cubans. His life would not be safe one moment without his soldiers within call. There have been all kinds of ridiculous reports in circulation here among the Spaniards in regard to the thirty million bill, the sale of Cuba, etc., etc. One of the most ridiculous is this—"a Spanish gentleman of undoubted authority," called a few days since on the Captain General, who in the course of private conversation, showed him an autographed letter from President Buchanan, offering to bribe Concha with thirty million dollars to declare the island independent of the Spanish crown, and promising a much larger sum to have him subsequently cede it to the United States. The most improbable part of this was that if any such bribe could be offered, Concha would undoubtedly have accepted it, and not shown such a letter. But the aforesaid Spanish gentleman (of <u>undoubted authority</u>) added that General Concha indignantly spurned such [a] base offer, and would never suffer the <u>honor</u> of the Spanish nation to be tarnished by any act of his. Still I hardly think it would be safe, for any administration to make any such kind of an offer to bribe, without it was expected to have it accepted. When Concha succeeded to the command of the island, he made his appearance like a conqueror, surrounded by a large army, composed wholly of Spanish-born subjects, he evidently expected to find the island in a state of revolt, and anticipated a fight before getting a foothold on land. His efforts have been ever since to impress the home government with the idea that he is suppressing the fires of a volcano, and his dreams are manifestly of conspiracies, murder and filibusters. He has either a lack of judgement or courage, not to perceive that the whole people of Cuba are averse to Spanish rule, though but very few men have as yet seriously endeavored to overthrow it. His salary was a few years since increased by the government at Madrid, from twenty thousand to fifty thousand dollars a year, to compensate him for certain fees which his predecessors had enjoyed besides their salary, and which he renounced. He had also promised in anticipation of this increased salary to use his utmost efforts to break up the slave trade. How he has lived up to his professions is well known, for there are probably from twenty to forty cargoes of slaves landed each year in different parts of the island, and there may be one or two vessels intercepted by the authorities

during the year which cases are made very public, for a <u>show</u> of vigilance, etc. General Concha is
rarely seen in the streets of Havana, and then always accompanied by his bodyguard of a hundred
or so of lancers. I have seen him once at the theatre, and once at Mass, both times strongly
guarded. He is a gentlemanly looking man apparently about fifty years of age, with hair partly gray,
and a heavy moustache. He has not the personal
appearance of a brave man, but seems low spir-
ited or melancholy, and apparently is always uneasy, and looking anxiously about himself. It is
said since the discovery of the conspiracy to as-
sassinate him at the theatre, he always wears a suit
of light steel armor under his clothing. "Uneasy
lies the head that wears a crown," etc. If he has
any such thing as a <u>conscience</u> about him, the
memory of his inhuman <u>murder</u> of fifty <u>unarmed</u>
American citizens just outside of Fort Atares must
haunt him fearfully.

We learned just at night that the *Cahawba* was
coming into port direct from New York. John H.
and myself went out to her anchorage in Rademin's boat to get late papers, etc. The same performance was gone through with as when I arrived
in the *Empire City* six weeks since. The boats of
the health officer and the customhouse with the
royal colors streaming from their sterns. After they
had satisfied themselves as to the *Cahawba* and her
passengers, we had permission to go on board
with others. <u>Such</u> a confusion—the swarthy boat-
men stripped to the waist generally, all jabbering
in an unknown tongue and soliciting the passengers to land in their boats. The water was covered

with fruit boats, selling oranges, bananas and other tropical fruits to the poor devils who have just come from a snow storm in New York. Returning, we pick our way through crowds of vessels, Yankee clippers predominating, and make our way to the customhouse wharf, about a mile from the steamer <u>anchorage</u>. We saw Purser Rogers (a Connecticut man) and Captain Bullock on board the steamer and ashore during the evening. About eight o'clk we went up to the Plaza d'Armas to hear the band play. The plaza was crowded with gaily dressed señoras and señoritas and their cavaliers promenading inside the enclosures while the surrounding streets were jammed with volantes, carriages, etc. We met in Dominicas several friends, Americans and others, and, after a quiet lunch and a good cigar, we strolled around the <u>Alameda d'Paula</u> in the glorious moonlight, and to bed about eleven o'clk pretty much used up with fatigue.

Saturday, March 19

RECEIVED SEVERAL LETTERS from home and from New York this morning, also Frank Leslie's pictorial with the views and descriptions of the Sickles tragedy and files of the *New York Herald*. John and self have been travelling all over Havana today, seeing the sights and making purchases, among others—some dresses, fans, etc., for Dora. We all dined with Mr. and Mrs. Ruchman today and had a very pleasant time. Mr. R. is a German who has resided here for many years. He is <u>anti</u>-filibuster and strongly supports the existing government of the island. Here of course we disagreed, but I found him a very intelligent and well informed gentleman, and he gave me a great deal of information on every subject relating to the island. In talking about the Lopez expedition, etc., I learned many facts which I can depend upon as authentic. Mr. R. was at the time of the last fatal expedition, president of the German charitable association here and received liberty from Concha to visit the condemned prisoners during their last hours and witnessed the execution. There were among Crittenden's party who were butchered on the hillside at Fort Atares, eight of his own countrymen, and he remained with them to the last, taking last messages and letters to families and friends at home. He tells me they were led out by tens, and <u>made to kneel with their backs to the soldiers,</u> who shot them down like dogs, and where they were not killed at the first fire a reserve marched up and putting the muzzles of the muskets close to their head blew out their brains. After twenty had been thus butchered, Colonel Crittenden and his second in command, Captain ———, were brought out, but they refused to kneel and they were forced and tied down, but at the moment of firing Crittenden broke his fastenings and stood upright and received the bullets through his body. He faced about with an expression of defiance, and was finally dispatched by half a dozen more shots. The other thirty were led out close by the side of their murdered comrades and dispatched by tens. Mr. R. says they all died like brave men, but he denies that their remains were subjected to any indignities from the rabble who witnessed the execution, but that the bodies were put into respectable hearses and carried to the Campo Santo (Holy Ground) and buried in that portion which is said to be unhallowed and used for heretics. He said however that some portions of skulls, blood, and brains, which were scattered around this place of slaughter, were scraped together by some of the low negroes, etc., and exhibited in the public places in the city, but it was discountenanced by the authorities as soon as known. I asked Mr. R. how it was that the Spanish force of twenty-five hundred men under General Eta attacked Lopez with his 300 half-armed men and boys and was defeated and terribly cut up losing their leader. He replied that the Spanish troops tried to force the filibusters from an almost impregnable position, and that they were said to be unerring marksmen and armed with very superior weapons. He told me also of seeing eighteen others of Lopez' companions taken in the woods near Las Pozas, who were tried by drumhead court-martial, and sentenced to be shot in one hour. Through the intercession of Mr. R., they each received a good supper which he says they all ate heartily, for they were half starved, having eaten nothing but berries, etc., for some days, and then they were led out and shot in the woods and shot by the light of a lantern, and their bodies left to be interred by any one who would dare to bury them, or else the turkey buzzards would soon dispose of them. That <u>retribution</u> will follow such cold-blooded murders is certain, and the future must settle all these things. I visited the hill of Atares this evening and was shown the spot where Colonel Crittenden and his unfortunate companions were sacrificed, and I looked about for the monument erected to their memory by two American gentlemen, an account of which I lately saw in a New Orleans paper, but no such monument was there and I question if it was ever erected—if so it has been removed. The time will come when the grateful State or Republic of Cuba will erect monuments sacred to the memory and to perpetuate the brave deed and heroic death of her first martyrs to liberty. I removed my baggage to Mrs. Almy's Hotel today and have for a roommate, Captain Murdock from San Nicolas. He is a brother-in-law of Mr. King and was well acquainted with George D'Wolf and family. He is very sociable but <u>rather</u> inclined to exaggerate in his statements. Mr. King is here also and a very quiet old gentleman. Mr. K. is a brother of the late Vice-President King. We visited the <u>Baños d' Mer</u>, or sea baths, which are cut out of solid rock just outside the walls beyond the presidio. Each bath has a hole cut so as to allow the seawater to flow in and out with the tide, and small enough to prevent sharks from entering. The floors are covered with clean hard white sand, and they are free to all. There are different departments for men, women and negroes and there is no reason why the "<u>great unwashed</u>" here should <u>not</u> wash and be clean. The temperature 70° of the water scarcely changes through the year, the waters of the Gulf Stream, running close along the shore here and washing the shores of the island. I presume this will account for the even temperature of the climate here.

It is a curious sight to see the long trains of mules and ponies coming into the city every morning tied one after the other (nose to tail) and each heavily loaded with cane and corn leaves piled on so thick that the animal can scarcely be seen. Many also with large panniers on each side filled with oranges, bananas, [and] sugarcane, and the drivers crying out their goods in an unknown tongue in their drawling singing way. All the morning these cries may be heard going by the hotel, a free translation of them would sound queer to American ladies. The style of numbering the streets and residences here very naturally puzzles a stranger as I found out today in looking for the office of Torice Puente and Co. The numbers commence at one end of a street, and go on, with one entire side in regular rotation to the termination of the street, then go back and take the opposite side in the same manner. Very few places of business have the names or firm over the door, but some fanciful title of which I believe I have written before. John Henry returned home this evening in the Cardenas steamer at eight o'clk. We accompanied him to the boat and I was really sorry to part with him for we have spent many pleasant hours together on the island. I hope to meet him again, however, both here and in the States. After he left I went to my old evening resort, the Plaza d'Armas, to hear the band play as usual and feeling rather lonesome came back to the hotel and went to bed before ten o'clk. I saw yesterday the first rain since I came to Cuba. We had a hurri-

cane of wind and torrents of rain for half an hour
or so.

Sunday, March 20

S UNDAY IN HAVANA is hardly to be distinguished
from any other day of the week excepting that
by most of the people here it is observed as a holiday. Nearly all the stores are open, and business
goes on as usual. In the afternoon, everybody able
to own or hire a volante or carriage goes out to
ride on the Paseo Isabel Segundo, where all the
beauty and fashion of Havana may be seen going
in files up one side of the paseo and down on
the other, the carriages being kept in line by a
mounted guard of lancers in their showy yellow
uniforms and cocked hats. Occasionally a fast
American breaks the line, and dashes down the
avenue with a "two forty" horse and skeleton
buggy, and the guard and crowd generally clear
the track. Good Spaniards complain that these
wild barbarian Yankees are about half-horse and
it [is] as well not to try to stop them. However
such fast amusements are done at the risk of a visit
to the Moro Castle, and is a luxury not often to be
indulged in. The paseo's are lined with a double
row of royal palm trees, and fountains playing at
short distances. This being "Holy Week," there are
less amusements than at any other time during
Lent, but I notice by the Diario this morning that
two theaters are open this evening, besides several concerts etc., and the celebrated Snake Man,
from the United States, exhibits his famous

collection of serpents from all parts of the world. This fellow is a <u>slick</u> Yankee rejoicing in the title of <u>colonel</u>, and he is "doing" the Cubanos out of their dollars by showing his snakes alive and dead, and (through an interpreter) telling the most wonderful stories in regard to their habits, and all of which seem to be swallowed by the admiring audience with as much gusto, as the boa constrictor disposes of the rabbit. This <u>colonel</u> (I forget his name) has made a tour of the island, and has coined money, as the exhibition is a novelty in these parts, snakes being scarce articles in this country. At <u>Guines</u> the other day the anaconda escaped from his cage, and glided gracefully around among the audience who "<u>vamosed the rancho</u>" instanter. At Cardenas he lost a great portion of his preserved snakes, as the cases took fire, and the snakes being kept in alcohol, were soon thoroughly cooked and thus were spoiled for exhibition. At the latter place I saw while there, Mr. Nellis, the man without arms, who is charming the people of that locality by his skill in using his toes in the place of fingers. Nellis says he likes the Dons, and he modestly charges them <u>only dos pesos</u> each ($2) for showing them with what dexterity he can cut, write, sew, fire pistol, wind up watch, etc., etc., with his toes.

At present there are no bullfights (which I do not much regret as I have but little desire to see one) and cockfights are allowed only on Mondays but for a variety there was a <u>military Mass</u>, celebrated at the Belen church this morning. Getting up early I was fortunate enough to witness it—an entire regiment, all going through their religious genuflections, kneeling, crossing, bowing, etc., in a style that would have done credit to them on parade for professionals and uniformity. At the sound of the trumpet they marched out of church headed by the band playing the Spanish national air—King's March. The band is the "crack" band of the army hero, called the artillery band and it was something of a novelty to me. It consists of nearly one hundred members, and the arrangement of the different instruments was on an entirely new principle to me. In the front rank were about twenty brass bugles or trumpets, the succeeding rank about as many brass drums, then a line of trombones, then horns or cornets, and, lastly, clarionets and cymbals. The music was loud and "brassy" and might be heard for miles. The Spanish seem to have a peculiar fancy for noise, in everything connected with military, and the braying of the brazen trumpets, the roll of the little brass drums, and the firing of guns may be heard every hour in all parts of the city, day, and night. At every military station, guardhouse, and barracks, (and I have noticed over fifty of such localities), the guard is changed every hour, and then their loaded muskets are discharged. The men-of-war in the harbor are also continually saluting, practicing, etc., and firing signal guns, and thus a large quantity of powder is burned daily. I doubt if the "smell of powder" renders these brave defenders more brave. The Cubans, however, foot the bills.

I stepped into the old cathedral again this morning to have another look at the tomb of Columbus. It was early but quite a number of persons were attending Mass. With other Americans and strangers, I strolled around the building examining the magnificent paintings, statuary, etc., and watching the pretty señoritas as they <u>bobbed</u> up and down, as the little bell was sounded by the priest's attendant. In the churches here all are equal, the wealthy hidalgo and the ragged negro all kneel down together on the marble pavement, for there are no pew[s] with luxurious cushions, but I notice most of the wealthy people are attended by servants, who carry rugs, carpets, etc., for them to kneel up on without spoiling their dresses. The figures of the saints and of Christ are lifesize and of wax, and dressed in the most extravagant style being covered with jewels and costly ornaments.

The harbor today presents a beautiful appearance, such a spectacle as I never before witnessed. The flags of all the shipping being displayed and I can see from the balcony of our hotel the flags of nearly every maritime nation. Conspicuous are the <u>stars and stripes</u>, and the red cross of St. George, the sickly looking flag of Spain with its broad yellow stripes, reminding one of quarantine and yellow fever—also the tri-color of France; the black and double headed eagles of Austria, Russia, and Prussia—the flag of Hamburg, and of some of the South American republics, but it is especially gratifying to an American to see, that at least two-thirds of all the shipping in the harbor, carry the flag of our glorious union at their mast head, and yet the American has been the least respected or feared by the government here of any flag that flies at Havana. Some of our naval force should be stationed here, for American interests need protection quite as much as those of other nations. Eighteenth letter to *Times* today, giving my ideas of Sunday in Havana. The public hospital of San Juan de Dios (St. John of God) is well worthy of the notice of a stranger here. I passed some time in visiting it and was amply repaid. It is a large, plain building with nothing particularly attractive in its appearance. A sentinel was on guard at the door and a few paces further in sat the mayordomo or porter at his desk. On passing through the gateway we come to a quite spacious square, in which are growing some beautiful tropical flowers and plantain and coconut trees. Among the flowers, I notice fuschias, oleanders, roses, and many of whose names I am ignorant. A double gallery runs all around the inside of the building and faces this open square. We passed through several of the wards, which were clean and neat furnished with single iron bedstead, some with canvas bottoms only and others with good mattresses. I saw some two or three hundred beds, but I believe the building has accommodations for one thousand patients. And all who I saw were evidently well cared for. There were numerous nurses, and all under the direction of the "Sisters of Charity," several of whom reside permanently in the hospital. In passing one of these estimable sisters I raised my hat and the salutation was gracefully returned with a quiet elegance which proved her a lady in my estimation. The fact of these sisters having the superintendence of this hospital accounts for the universal neatness and cleanliness which prevails here. In one of the numerous rooms I saw a little altar fancifully fitted up and a priest at his devotions. He is permanently attached to the hospital.

I notice here that patients with yellow fever are not separated from the others, and the attending physicians assure me that it is an established fact, and universally admitted among the "medicos" here that yellow fever is <u>not</u> contagious.

The Spaniards may be cruel to slaves and I believe they are so, but here in this hospital at least all are equally well cared for—black and white, and I could not see the slightest difference in the accommodations of the two races. All were in clean beds and all received the same attention.

Monday, March 21

DURING LENT cockfights are only allowed on Mondays, and the <u>genteel</u> place for this intellectual amusement is at the village of Guanabacoa about three miles from Havana. Van Cortlandt and myself took the cars on the new Matanzas railroad at the terminus of the Regla ferry and visited the place this morning and found it a <u>first class</u> cockpit, which is licensed by government or rather by the Captain Generals and presided over by the <u>Gobernador</u> of Guanabacoa.

The pit is a circle of some twenty-five feet in diameter, surrounded by a close railing, three feet high, behind which are the seats for spectators, raising in tiers nearly to the roof of the building, which is circular and capable of holding three or four hundred persons. Those of all shades of color were present: white, black, lemon and mahogany color, mixed indiscriminately, all shouting and greatly excited by the prospect of the fight, while the conversation was anything <u>but</u> edifying to a disinterested spectator. All seem to command and nobody obeyed, but finally the pit was cleared, the cocks weighted and pitted, and the bell struck for the entertainment to commence. Two men were in the pit who are called <u>galleros,</u> or persons whom the owners of the cocks give the care of their champions while the fight is going on. The fights were long and stubborn, the birds seeming to have great endurance; and as they are not allowed to wear steel gaffs, and fight only with the naked spur, the result is seldom fatal in either cock. We saw three matches in each of which a white cock was beaten, the red and black winning the fight. These red and black cocks are a cross of English and Spanish game fowls, and said to be a very superior class. During the fight, when the birds became exhausted, the <u>galleros</u> would take the birds up, and revive and encourage them by wiping the blood carefully away from their heads and necks, and spiriting mouthfuls of spirits over its head and body and blowing it down the throat, smoothing the ruffled feathers, and occasionally putting the fowl's head in their mouths(!) and sucking blood from its wounds. They were then put down again and the fight continued until one of them was vanquished. The meaning of the shouts and howls I understood but little of, but knew that it meant offers to bet, and shouts of encouragement to the different fowl.

The cockpit was a perfect pandemonium, and all were equal there—white and black, slave and free—all betting, drinking, and smoking together. It would have rejoiced the heart of the most ardent abolitionists to see the perfect familiarity between the two races.

I was fortunate enough to witness a marriage ceremony in the old cathedral this morning. It is very similar to our Episcopal service, adding only the Communion service, in which all present join. For legitimate marriages here, the consent of the parents is required if any are living, otherwise some "official," who thus signifies to the lawful age, etc., of the parties. If either party passes any title or belongs to the army or navy, a royal license is required.

Priests and nuns are not allowed to marry, but widowers with children even, are permitted to become priests. As priests cannot legally marry, they cannot of course have any legitimate children, but it is a notorious fact that a great many often have a quantum sufficit of young nieces and nephews. In Catholic countries marriage is at the same time a contract and a sacrament, and does not end until the death of one of the parties. Complete divorce never takes place, but a temporary separation is sometimes granted, that is, so long as the causes which occasioned it are not removed. Whether this system encourages or diminishes morality, I am unable to say. I think the statistics would show the latter to be the case.

This evening while sitting in Reichman's house, we saw the passing of El Sanctissimo. Persons on the near approach of death receive the sacrament in their beds with imposing ceremonies. The friends or relatives of the sick person walk from the church to the house with head uncovered, and burning wax candles in their hands, on both sides of the volante in which the priest takes the <u>Very Holy</u>, and the procession is preceded by a boy, ringing a bell to give notice of its approach. It is the custom of many not to use a new carriage or volante until it has been once employed in this kind of procession, and received the blessing of the officiating priest. All persons meeting the procession in the streets (from the Captain General down to the lowest negro) must kneel down, and those riding in carriages, stop, get out, and go down on their knees also. The people in their houses all along the route do the same, bearing lighted candles to their windows and balconies, while the procession is passing. If it passes a guard room, some of the soldiers join them, reverse muskets and beat the dead march as long as the carriage remains in sight. In the room of the sick person a temporary altar is erected for the performance of the service, while the room is ornamented in the best possible manner, decorated with flowers, etc. The room is filled with friends all bearing lighted candles, and kneeling while the Communion is administered. The procession then returns to the church in the same manner but by a different route, so as to make the ceremony as imposing and public as possible. Wrote nineteenth and twentieth letter to *Times* today. Shopping today, buying cigars, some fans, and few articles for presents, etc., at home. On the plaza as usual this evening. Several ladies of my acquaintance called at Mrs Almy's this evening, and we spent an hour very pleasantly.

Tuesday, March 22

Expected the steamer *Empire City* all day, she being due from New Orleans, and this morning the telegraph on the Moro announced an American steamer in the offing and everybody of course supposed it to be the *Empire* so I notified Anita to be ready to go on board this evening and commenced packing up my own traps, but two hours after it was found that it was the English steamer from St. Thomas, so we are still waiting for <u>our</u> steamer. When I first landed I knew less of the language than I now do (which is little enough) and consequently did not understand the many phrases uttered in my presence but I have learned since and now see that I rarely pass a crowd of Spaniards, particularly soldiers or sailors without hearing [an] insulting remark referring to me personally as an "Americano," so great is the hatred of the lower class of Spaniards to everything American.

Today Van C. and myself were walking outside the walls near the Tacon Theater (on the <u>Paseo Tacon</u>) when we were outrageously insulted by a couple of soldiers off duty. I explained to him and returned and demanded a retraction, at the same time enforcing our demand by certain movements of our canes, indicating a <u>forcible demonstration</u>. We were answered in the very humblest manner, and offered that it was a mistake probably owing to our imperfect knowledge of Spanish language. We were satisfied, however, that our interpreters (cudgels), solved the difficulty. The Cubans, on the other hand, are kind and obliging to foreigners, and they more especially exert themselves to please Americans. The Spaniards are not only as a nation, cowards, but like all cowards are most inveterate boasters, and the discovery of the new world is one of the feats most extolled by them. But history tells us that if their vessels did reach these islands before those of other nations it was in spite of the efforts of the Spaniards, who followed the illustrious Genoese, and who in their villainy and cowardice intended to compel him to return, and threatened to throw him overboard if he refused. The probable failure of this premeditated crime was on account of a <u>great fear</u>, as they were utterly ignorant of the art of navigation, and could not have returned without the assistance of the great discoverer. If Columbus had not been accustomed to despise Spanish boasting, or if he had feared their threats, there can be no doubt that the discovery would have been made by other nations, as he would have returned to Spain without effecting it. It has been truly said that "Spaniards, fortunately for their pride, forget all historical particulars, which tend to impair in the least the glory of their nation." It will be recollected that Columbus died at Valldolid in 1506, and in 1513 his remains were transferred to Seville, preparatory to their being sent (as desired in his will) to St. Domingo. When that island was ceded to France, the remains were delivered to the Spaniards—this was in 1796, and they were brought to Havana in a national ship, and were deposited in the cathedral, in the presence of all the high authorities. The cathedral itself, aside from this prominent feature of interest, is vastly attractive from its venerable character and appearance, and the visitor cannot but linger with pleasure and thoughtfulness among its marble aisles and confessionals. It is situated on the <u>Calle de Ignacio</u> (street of Ignacio) and its massive towers and pillared front defaced by time and covered with moss, recalls associations of past centuries. It is ornamented internally with fine old paintings, some of them of very great value and antiquity. The <u>great</u> object of interest here is a marble tablet set in the wall at the right of the great altar, having cut up on it the images of Columbus—this tablet forms the entrance to the tomb where rests all that is mortal of the discoverer of the Western World.

Many young Creoles and Spaniards visit the States each year, and represent themselves as belonging to a titled family, or the sons of wealthy planters, etc., and it seems to be a weakness of some of our northern girls to fancy a "furriner," especially if he is personally attractive and speaks English broken into very small pieces. I know of two or three cases, where young ladies of beauty and refinement have become so fascinated with these adventurers as to marry them, and on coming out to Cuba, find a father or mother-in-law of too dark a complexion to pass for even a Spaniard, in fact a mulatto or negro. Many planters have wives and mistresses of half or even whole negro blood, and as they are by law bound to provide for the issue of such union, there are many families who pride themselves on the respectability of their wealth and position, who have negro blood in their veins. Our northern ladies cannot be too particular, and can by a little observation, easily distinguish the difference between negro and Moorish complexions.

The Cubans are gradually getting into the ways and ideas of American life. A few years since an American horse and vehicle was a novelty here, but now, an American barouche, buggy, or hack is nearly as common on the paseo as the unwieldy volantes. American horses too, are all the rage, and the young buck[s] delight in displays of horsemanship, on fast trotting, but hard riding horses. The little Cuban ponies, so easy and graceful, are now out of fashion in Havana, and the larger a man's income now, the larger horse he drives. We occassionally see on the paseo a light skeleton buggy, drawn by a pair of thoroughbreds driven at full speed by some go-ahead Yankee, and then it is a good plan for volantes, horsemen and mounted police all to clear the track, for young America will drive fast without regard to the consequences.

I have visited within two or three days past several manufactories of cigars (tabacos they are called here) and do not find them to differ materially from ours at the north. The different qualities of tobacco are very carefully selected, and the cigars assorted according to color. I am satisfied that but very few of what are called here "the flowers," a first quality of cigars ever reach the States. Nearly all the large factories have orders in advance of the crop for cigars for the English clubhouses. For the best quality the most extravagant prices are asked and given. I bought a few boxes of an excellent mild cigar for $18 per thousand, and a couple of thousand of Conchas for a friend at $35 for, that would readily sell for $50 in New York. The thirty percent duties make up the prices on cigars (imported from here), in the States. I visited also the larger concern of C.R. Susina and Co. for the making of cigarros or cigarettes, where there is a business done of some $800,000 per annum. I paid for a box of one hundred bunches $2.80 and the[y] were the best. These articles are quite as generally used here as cigars and are much less expensive where smoking is so universal.

The expense of living on the island may average high to the stranger who has no friends or acquaintances in the country, though permanent residents here say the expense of living here in town, or country, all things considered is not more than in the States. The great item of fuel is dispensed with, except for culinary purposes, and clothing, being nearly all of linen or cotton, is of much less cost than woolen, though a much larger wardrobe is needed than in our climate. The luscious fruits and healthy vegetables in innumerable variety form a great share of provision of the table, and these can always be bought at the door for a trifling sum, and there is no occasion to lay by any quantity as the market supply never ceases. At the best hotels and boarding houses of Havana and Matanzas, the charge is three and half dollars a day unless a special contract is made for some length of time. In country towns at the tavernos the charge for entertainment for man and beast is of course very much less. Wines and cordials are at least fifty percent cheaper than in the States.

The Spanish and creole style of cooking, where nearly every dish is strongly flavored with onion or garlic and spiced with cayenne pepper, might not suit our Yankee palettes, but one soon gets accustomed to it, and as for myself, I really like it better than our plain cooking in the North. Olives and olive oil, sardines, chorr-chorr pickles, mustard, and the like delicacies and condiments all disappear rapidly at the Spanish table and there is no lack of the Catalan or red wine which is not intoxicating except it be in immoderate quantities but quenches the thirst admirably when mixed with <u>agua</u>.

Wednesday, March 23

V AN CORTLAND and myself started out at five o'clk this morning on a visit to the Moro, Cabanas, and Punta Forts. We <u>finished</u> the three fortifications by nine o'clk and returned to Madame Almy's in time for breakfast. We <u>took</u> the Punta Fort at <u>reveille</u>. It is a small affair directly opposite the Moro on the south side of the entrance of the harbor and mounts I think about fifty guns. In the vault under the fort is kept the <u>garrote</u>, the fatal chair on which Lopez, Pinto, and Estrampes, and other brave but unfortunate men have suffered martyrdom for the cause of liberty in this despotic country. The place of execution is on the sandy point just outside the fort and near the new prison buildings.

We took a boat from the water gate and worked over to the Moro just as the garrison were being mustered for parade and inspection. By the exercise of a little politeness and <u>considerable assurance</u> we obtained permission from the officer in command of the gate to enter and examine the castle. It is a <u>fine looking</u> piece of masonry, built upon solid rock foundation, but I noticed the walls are composed of limestone and rocks of coral formations, being quite soft and friable. Also that a great portion which appear very strong and grand from the harbor, is plaster work mixed with old tiles and whitewashed handsomely, but hardly able to resist the <u>influence</u> of mortars and Dahlgren guns. The armament of the castle is very extensive, but the guns are mostly dismounted and the ammunition is sealed up in ovens of masonry to protect it from the moisture and salt water, for in a heavy <u>norther</u>, the waves frequently dash over the walls of the castle, rendering the barracks and quarters <u>somewhat</u> damp. I should judge however that water would not materially damage a Spanish soldier (especially if it could be combined with soap). Some of the guns are of great size, and made of fine bell metal, and some, I believe contain a quantity of silver in their composition. There <u>appeared</u> to be a plentiful supply of munitions of war in the shape of bombs, balls, and grenades, and I should judge there was a garrison of some three hundred men. The soldier's quarters looked clean (outside) and were well ventilated, but the <u>soldiers</u> (heaven save the name) were the most ill favored, clownish looking set, I ever saw in uniform. Short in stature and with a clumsy, swinging gait as they marched. I hardly saw one who <u>looked</u> of ordinary intelligence. They had low foreheads to a man, and vulgar, brutal looking faces. State prison convicts at Wethersfield in their parti-colored uniform appear to much better advantage. The officers seem to be generally of a very different class and are gentlemanly and polite to strangers. We were allowed to go up to the telegraph station and from there to the top of the lighthouse which is a fine stone structure inside the walls of the castle and was erected by Captain General O'Donnell in 1844. The view from the lighthouse is unsurpassed in Cuba. The city harbor of Havana can be seen at a glance, and the white walls of the fortification, around the city, were glistening in the rays of the morning sun, which was just rising as we reached the summit. Looking inland the eye reaches over a vast extent of level country looking green and beautiful with the ever waving palm, standing guard over the surrounding fields. The view toward the sea is grand, and on a clear day the Florida Keys can be distinctly seen with the aid of a glass. We counted about twenty sail[s] coming in, from a Prussian ninety gun frigate down to a little Yankee schooner scudding before the morning breeze. Right from under the walls came fast a trim looking mail steamer with our flag flying and at first we supposed it to be the *Empire City*, due yesterday, but a second glance at her size, engine, etc., convinced me to the contrary and we soon ascertained her to be the steamer *Granada* from [. . .].

On descending into the fort we were allowed by the officer who admitted us to look at the different kinds of arms used, Minie rifles, etc., and as we took an interest in these matters, we became quite sociable with our kind entertainer, and although we avowed ourselves <u>Americanos</u> and <u>filibusteros</u>, he refused to believe it, with the characteristic shrug, and offered to show us the dungeons, etc., below, and the subterranean passage to the Cabanas. Want of time obliged us to decline, and he gave us a <u>recommendado</u> to the officer commanding the gate of the Cabanas fortress. We made a hasty run thro' the Cabanas, and as the sun was getting warm we took a boat soon for the other side and <u>made</u> for our hotel. The Cabanas is much larger than the Moro, and when fully manned, requires a garrison of two thousand men. I think it mounts about three hundred guns. It is in about the same condition as the Moro and built in a similar style, and protected in the rear by a succession of batteries rising up one above the other, on the hills. But I doubt not a few Yankees, with our Engineer Corps, could capture both these famous forts, in a few days at most; and these command Havana and the neighboring fortifications. But I will leave this subject to be discussed by those who better understand it, but one thing we all know, that if an American force landed here with the intention of capturing these famous forts, it would be accomplished in the time prescribed by the commanding officer. Have been busy all day having a <u>last look</u> at all the lions of Havana, and calling on some few friends I have made here saying "<u>adios</u>," for our steamer will surely be here within a few hours.

While walking on the <u>Alameda d' Paula</u> this afternoon I saw the <u>stars and stripes</u> on the telegraph station at the Moro. I ran down by customhouse wharf, and just arrived in time to see <u>two</u> American steamers sail slowly up the harbor. First came the *Illinois* crowded with passengers from California, having put in here disabled, and, close behind came our old friend the *Empire City*, steaming up bravely, and the tall form of Captain Griffin standing on the quarter deck. I cheer with the crowd as they passed and jumping into a <u>bota</u> ordered the man to pull out to the anchorage. Waiting for the Everlasting Health and customhouse officers. I was on board by five o'clk and shaking hands with Captain Griffin and Purser Denison. I was greatly surprised to meet an old friend from Boston (Ned Ives) on the way from New Orleans to New York to finish up his wedding tour. Spent half an hour agreeably and then ashore to <u>pack up</u>. Went over to Reichman's and notified Cousin Anita to be ready by seven o'clk in the morning as I wish to be on board early although the steamer does not sail until ten o'clk or after. Tonight Havana is full of Americans, as there [are] four American steamers in port—the *Isabel, Granada, Illinois,* and *Empire City*. The Illinois has about five hundred returning Californians, and they are all "bound to come ashore," so the plaza, Dominica's, and all places of public resort are completely filled by our "northern barbarians." When such a rush comes in, the customhouse authorities have great difficulty in enforcing the regulations concerning landing permits, etc., and many come and go paying no attention to them. The Spanish officials are cautioned always to avoid much interference with California transit passengers as they are, sometimes rather troublesome customers even here.

Went up to the plaza with Van C. for the last time, and walked round and round getting a parting glance at the señoritas, and the last rounds of the artillery band playing the "Anvil Chorus." Saw our Captain Griffin promenading with a lady on each arm and met several American acquaintances at Dominica's—among others—Miss Wood, who was a passenger with us coming out.

Thursday, March 24

M Y LAST MORNING in Havana. Up early and took a long walk outside the walls, returning by the Plaza D'Armas and the market. The novelty of everything here compared with what I shall see in New York a few days hence now comes over me and I realize it as forcibly as I did when I first landed in Havana. The narrowness of the streets scarce a dozen feet wide and the exceedingly narrow walks so poorly adapted for crinoline and the hooped skirts or "malakoffs" as they are called here. Then the peculiar Moorish style of house, mostly one story high, massively built, with stuccoed walls with all the shades of the rainbow for coloring. Some with overhanging balconies rudely ornamented, and with huge front doors, studded with ponderous iron spikes and the iron barred and grated windows, reminding me that the days when these buildings were erected were different from the present day.

Numbers of country people (guajiros) and now and then a stalwart and swarthy negro leading little scrawny mules, that looked ready to break down under their ponderous loads of fruit and vegetables, sometimes piled upon the poor little animal so that only his ears and feet were visible to the passerby. The water carriages too with a brace of kegs on either side of the mule's back and the great lazy owner astride the haunches of the unlucky but patient brute. Crowds of soldiers hurrying toward the barracks for morning parade, and occasionally a burly priest with his long black gown and broad shovel hat passed by, or a party of shrivelled old women with piercing black eyes, occasionally accompanied with some pretty little señorita, with her <u>reboza</u> thrown gracefully over head all on the way to Mass.

I managed to get Señorita Anita and all her <u>traps</u> onboard before eight o'clk, and after a little chaffering with the customhouse officer on the wharf, managed to get off all my baggage, cigars, baskets of oranges, packages of cane sweet-meats, etc., without passing them through the customhouse.

Last evening in company with some American acquaintances (just about returning home), I took an evening ride out through <u>the Paseo Isabel Segunda</u> and the <u>Cerro</u>. We stopped on these avenues to visit beautiful residences and gardens of the Bishop of Havana, the Marquis Santovenia and the Count Fernandina. The charming wife of the latter gentleman is a great friend of all Americans and has the reputation of being at heart a strong <u>filibustero</u>. On our asking permission to enter the grounds, she sent us word that the premises were always open to American <u>gentlemen</u>, and after going through the magnificent gardens loaded with the perfume of a thousand tropical flowers and fruits, we found on passing out a bountiful supply of fruit, wine, etc., prepared for us at the porter's lodge, and an invitation to call again and bring our friend. This is true Cuban hospitality.

We rode back to the city just as the gates were closing for the night. An evening or night ride here can but impress the sojourner that he is really a stranger in a strange land. The sky seems clearer, the stars shine brighter, and the moonlight seems to penetrate the atmosphere as it never does at the North. The constellation of stars called the "Southern Cross" never greets our eyes at home, but here, by it the traveller can find his way with unerring certainty. At midnight the cross stands erect, and after that hour has passed, the cross declines. Humboldt says he has often heard the herdsmen in South America say—"Midnight is past—the cross begins to bend." It is called by the Spaniards "Cruz d' Mayo" or Cross of May, as in that month it shines brightest and is most perfect.

Justice requires I should speak of the Hotel d' Luz conducted by Madame Almy, where I have been during my short stay in Havana. It is so different from every other pozada that I have seen in Cuba, that it deserves more than favorable mention. It is the favorite resort of Americans visiting the island and is deservedly popular. The location is good, being near the coastline of steamers, convenient to the customhouse, etc., close by the harbor and near that pleasant promenade the Alameda d' Paula. The rooms are neat and the beds sweet and clean (which is a rare luxury in this country) and the table well supplied with the fruits and vegetables of the tropics as well as the more substantial dishes of the North, and the guests naturally feel themselves at home.

Mrs. Almy is singularly fortunate in the selection of her "<u>major domo</u>" (or clerk of the house), in the person of <u>Henry Rademin</u>, who has the faculty of making himself useful and agreeable, and very soon well acquainted with every one stopping at the house. He is a German by birth, but speaks equally well with his native tongue, French, English, and Spanish, and often converses in three or four languages at the same time. He knows everybody and everything in Havana, <u>ergo</u> he is indispensable to the stranger. I would recommend any stranger visiting Havana to get into the good graces of "<u>Our Henry</u>."

At this hotel died the lamented <u>Doctor Kane</u>. I find by reference to the register of arrivals, that he came here December 26, 1856, and died Monday, July 16, 1857—a noble soul, regretted by all who ever knew him. Opposite the entry of his name is written, "The glories of our earthly estate and shadows—not substantial things"—and,

"To win the wreath of fame—
And to write on memory's scroll
A deathless name."

His death produced a remarkable sensation in Havana, and the funeral ceremonies were of such a nature as to render them very solemn and imposing.

The distant view of the *Empire City* just beginning to steam up, reminds me that in a few hours I must bid farewell to these delicious shores of Cuba, with all their features of enchantment, where all nature is beautiful, and where mere existence is a positive luxury. I might fill pages of statistics showing its wonderful fertility; but words cannot express or give adequate idea of what it is; it must be seen to be appreciated. What is needed here is an infusion of blood and nerve of a more enterprising and sterner race of men, and when its capabilities are fairly tested it will astonish the world with its productivity. Mr. Everett was right when he said, "This favored land wants nothing but <u>men</u> to turn its advantages to account, and enjoy their results, to be acknowledged as the <u>garden of the world</u>." My short stay here seems like a dream; but it is a dream of too bright things to be forgotten. The groves of oranges and palm, the odor of the thousand sweet flowers, the cool nights and sunny days of the tropics, smiling skies and laughing waters, the volantes, military parades, the Plaza d'Armas, and the music of the splendid band each evening, the <u>paseo</u> and the bright eyed señoritas, the gardens and fountains—the beautiful harbor of Havana, guarded by its grim fortresses and batteries, and the country with broad fields of sugarcane and its gardens of coffee and tobacco—the long rides through the savannahs and thick woods loaded with the richest and choicest of flora's offerings— all these and a thousand other pleasant memories come trooping through the mind as my thoughts turn homeward. May I live to see this favored island represented by one of the galaxy of stars which glisten in the blue field of the flag of the free. The steamer was to sail at ten o'clk this morning (so the Captain had said) but with the usual dispatch of business at the customhouse, it was just twelve before our anchor was weighed and we steamed slowly down the harbor. We left the *Granada*, to follow us at three o'clk and the *Illinois* next day, also the *Isabel* for Charleston tomorrow morning.

The day was warm and beautiful and the sea smooth outside the Moro. Quite a number of passengers came on board at Havana, and Captain Griffin has several ladies onboard of his own family so I am in a great measure relieved of the care of my travelling companion, Señorita Anita. All the passengers were at the table, and our good steamer runs fast and promises a quick passage. We strike the Gulf Stream soon after leaving the Moro and just at night see lights on the Florida Coast. On deck in the evening until a late hour, and before retiring take one more last look at the "Southern Cross," for tomorrow evening it will be below our horizon. We have a pleasant party of passengers and all seem to enjoy themselves. My friend, Ned Ives, and self talk over old times when we lived in New Haven years ago, and of the many changes that have taken place since that time. We signal a steamer heading back to Havana supposed to be the *Philadelphia* from New York, but at such a distance as to render it uncertain, and turn in at six bells.

Friday, March 25

W E PASS GREAT NUMBERS of vessels nearly all bound north and with a good southerly breeze. Some motion of the ship this morning, consequently some of our passengers are in their berths instead of being on deck enjoying the air. A change of temperature since yesterday and I have changed linen clothing for thin woolen and cotton. While at dinner this afternoon we were struck suddenly by a "<u>norther</u>" which caused a general clearing of the table—most of the passengers and some of the crockery. However, I was blessed with an uncommon good appetite, and could not give up Captain Griffin's wine and an English plum pudding. I managed to deposit Anita in her berth, and after dinner went on deck to get a good view of the sea in a gale. It was a grand sight, and the water seemed alive. Huge waves dashed over our forward deck, but our tough old steamer dove through them and made her ten or eleven knots. The captain seemed contented and satisfied, so I was also—The gale increased till almost midnight and then the wind fell, but left the sea with a heavy swell. This was <u>uncomfortable</u> to say the least and I <u>turned in</u>, but I was not at all seasick but found some difficulty keeping in my berth being an upper one, and braced myself head and feet and did not venture to sleep much for fear of pitching out. Ives and his wife both sick and a great proportion of the passengers. Anita not much sick but <u>disinclined</u> to leave berth. I slept but little this night for my roommate was one of the sick ones, and his neighborhood was sometimes unpleasant for a full stomach like mine. I found however that while the ship rolled so much, that the settees and lounges in the cabin were preferable to the staterooms and availed myself of them accordingly.

Saturday, March 26

THE SEA [is] getting smooth again and by noon I regained my <u>sea legs</u> enough to walk the deck. I found my appetite holds good, and my seasickness which I expected does not come on. The weather grows cooler. I have doffed my panama hat and slippers, put on a cap, boots, thick cravat, and vest. We are steaming along at a fine rate and expect to make New York in five days at least. But few of our passengers get to the dinner table this noon, but Captain Griffin, myself, and a few others do justice to the dishes. I have become so accustomed to the motion of the ship that I trust myself in the barbers hands and get a comfortable shave without being cut either.

Having brought a supply of reading matter along with me from San Ricardo, I find no difficulty in passing away the time, and this evening the sea has become so calm that many of the lady passengers are on deck. I can imagine the folks at home sitting around the stove and the air here begins to feel tonight as if a little fire would not be unpleasant. We have quite a number of children on board, and they are almost a nuisance in the cabin, but I notice they do not seem to be troubled with seasickness at all, and play around in the roughest weather. If my own children were here I presume I should not consider <u>them</u> a nuisance.

Sunday, March 27

GROWING COOLER and this morning I put on my thick woolen underclothes, etc., and now begin to realize the March weather to which I am accustomed in New England. I can hardly realize that for some weeks past I have been enjoying a tropical winter, but now I am getting toward the reality of a northern spring. It has been cloudy all day, but the water is smooth and we steam along rapidly. The old *Empire City* does herself credit and Captain G., the purser, and all the officers predict a quick passage. An observation showed us to be off Cape Hatteras this noon and we passed it without a storm. The lighthouse was visible with a flag. This afternoon sitting on deck, I read the afternoon service from the prayer book, about the same time as the family at home would be reading the same in church. Everybody rather quiet aboard today, though we have no religious services on the steamer.

Monday March 28

COLD AND CLOUDY—overcoats needed and the little Spanish boy in the next stateroom to mine goes about the deck wrapped up in a blanket whining "mucho frio." Poor little fellow, he has not suitable clothing for a March day here, and will need attending too as soon as he gets ashore. We are progressing finely, making over two hundred eighty miles every twenty-four hours and if a storm does not come on we intend to be at the dock in New York before morning. We passed Barnegat light at three o'clk and by eight o'clk made Sandy Hook light. A pilot came aboard about nine and was of course besieged for late papers and news by the passengers. We find we have outstripped all the other steamers about due, and all hands on board are feeling merry, at the prospect of our voyage being ended so soon—a thick haze and fog is setting in and rain coming on, and we are fortunate for two hours later off the Hook we should have to put out to sea again. Our pilot however pushed along and at just twelve o'clk, we were made fast to the dock at the foot of Warren Street in New York. It was too late to go ashore tonight, and I willingly retired to my berth to sleep a few hours more on board [the] steamer and dream over the incidents of my trip to Cuba.

Bibliographical Essay: Selected Travel Titles

A vast amount of travel literature on Cuba written by North Americans appeared throughout the nineteenth century with the middle decades producing some of the richest selections. Visitors had different reasons for travel to Cuba: vacationers came to escape the northern latitudes during the winter months; scientists—most commonly referred to as "naturalists"—sought out the fauna and flora of the tropics; the sick came in search of the cures associated with the world-famous baths and mineral springs of the island; and businessmen arrived to invest or look after their investments.

Several travel accounts, written in the same year as Dimock's, offer interesting supplemental views of the island during 1859. Perhaps one of the most important published accounts of 1859 was Richard Henry Dana, Jr.'s *To Cuba and Back: A Vacation Voyage* (Boston, 1859), which is especially good for its description of Havana, Matanzas, and points in between. Another traveler to Cuba in 1859 was Anthony Trollope, who recounted his experiences in *The West Indies and the Spanish Main* (New York, 1860). Trollope traveled between Havana and Cienfuegos and recorded fascinating observations about slavery, amusements, and colonial administration. The Reverend John Stephens Cabot also visited Havana in 1859 and recorded his memoirs in *South and North; or Impressions Received during a Trip to Cuba and the South* (New York, 1860), which serves as a useful source on daily life in the capital. Jonathan S. Jenkins published a series of articles that appeared years later as "Life and Society in Old Cuba: Extracts from the Journal of Jonathan S. Jenkins, an American Painter of Miniatures, Written in 1859" in *Century Illustrated Monthly Magazine* 61 (1898): 742–52 and 941–57.

Among the most interesting published accounts written by women travelers, perhaps the most important is Mrs. Julia Ward, *A Trip to Cuba* (Boston, 1860). The frequently cited published journal deals thoroughly with such diverse matters as daily recreation forms, education, charity, restaurants, hotels, slavery, and agriculture. Also extremely useful is Eliza McHatton-Ripley, *From Flag to Flag: A Woman's Adventures and Experiences in the South during the War, in Mexico and in Cuba* (New York, 1889). McHatton-Ripley actually took up residence on the island after the U.S. Civil War in the late 1860s. She provides useful observations about rural life in Cuba. Amelia Mathilda Murray, *Letters from the United States, Cuba and Canada* (New York, 1857) recounts her travels to the island in 1855 and is especially good on commentary relating to Havana and Matanzas as well as on slavery and plantation life. Mrs. Rachel Wilson Moore, *The Journal of Rachel Moore Kept during a Tour to the West Indies and South America* (Philadelphia, 1867) recounts her impressions of a visit to Havana in 1863.

Some important published accounts focused on what could best be described as "health tourism." Physician Charles D. Tyng, *The Stranger in the Tropics: Being a Handbook for Havana and a Guidebook for Travellers to Cuba, Puerto Rico and St. Thomas* (New York, 1868) focuses on the springs and spas said to have possessed recuperative powers. Dr. Robert Wilson Gibbes published *Cuba for Invalids* (New York, 1860) in which he detailed the health benefits of extended visits to Cuba. One of the outstanding travel accounts of this period is Samuel Hazard, *Cuba With Pen and Pencil* (Hartford, 1871), which recounts his travel experiences in 1866 and gives considerable attention to health matters. Nathaniel Parker Willis, *Health Trip to the Tropics* (New York, 1853) recounts his visit to Cuba in 1852 with particular attention to mineral baths. An anonymous account titled *A Winter in the West Indies* (New York, 1839) describes Trinidad and Havana in the subtitle as "places of resort for northern invalids by an invalid." Physician John George F. Wurdemann wrote *Notes on Cuba* (Boston, 1844). He provides an account of his travels to Cuba in 1841, 1842, and 1843, and pays particular attention to Cuba as a site of recuperative possibilities.

Among other interesting travel accounts for these years is the published volume by the Reverend Robert Baird, *Impressions and Experiences of the West Indies and North America in 1849* (Philadelphia, 1850), which includes comments principally about Havana on such diverse themes as the press, the slave trade, religion, the judicial system, and cafés. In the same year, poet-journalist William Cullen Bryant traveled to Cuba. He published his impressions in *Letters of a Traveller, or Notes of Things Seen in Europe and America* (New York, 1855). Bryant was an astute observer and recorded impressions on a wide range of subjects including sugar plantations, coffee farms, slavery, attire, recreational forms, internal politics, and economic development. Several years later, Maturin Murray Ballou visited Cuba and published one of the outstanding travel accounts of the period. In *History of Cuba, or Notes of a Traveller in the Tropics Being a Political, Historical, and Statistical Account of the*

Island from Its First Discovery to the Present Time
(Boston, 1854), Ballou prepared a veritable encyclo-
pedia on Cuban daily life. One year after Dimock's visit,
John Milton Mackie traveled to Cuba and published
From Cape Cod to Dixie and the Tropics (New York,
1864). The Mackie account includes observations
about hotels, churches, railroad travel, and daily recreational forms.

Other useful travel accounts for this period include
Norman Benjamin Moore, *Rambles by Land and Water, or Notes of Travel in Cuba and Mexico* (New York,
1845) and Demoticus Philateles, *Yankee Travels
Through the Island of Cuba, or the Men and the Government, the Laws and Customs of Cuba as Seen by
American Eyes* (New York, 1856). The Reverend
James Rawson, *Cuba* (New York, 1857) chronicled his
travels in Cuba during the 1840s. Rawson pays particular attention to street scenes, churches, charity, and
climate. Richard Burleigh Kimball's *Cuba and the Cubans* (New York, 1850) is especially good for social
conditions in Havana. Carlton H. Roger visited Cuba
in 1856 and published *Incidents of Travel in the Southern States and Cuba* (New York, 1862). Alexander
Jones, *Cuba in 1851, Containing Authentic Statistics
of the Population, Agriculture and Commerce of the
Island* (New York, 1851) provides a summary of some
of the more important facets of midnineteenth-century
Cuba.

Latin American Silhouettes
Studies in History and Culture

William H. Beezley and
Judith Ewell
Editors

Volumes Published

William H. Beezley and Judith Ewell, eds., *The Human Tradition in Latin America: The Twentieth Century* (1987). Cloth ISBN 0-8420-2283-X Paper ISBN 0-8420-2284-8

Judith Ewell and William H. Beezley, eds., *The Human Tradition in Latin America: The Nineteenth Century* (1989). Cloth ISBN 0-8420-2331-3 Paper ISBN 0-8420-2332-1

David G. LaFrance, *The Mexican Revolution in Puebla, 1908–1913: The Maderista Movement and the Failure of Liberal Reform* (1989). ISBN 0-8420-2293-7

Mark A. Burkholder, *Politics of a Colonial Career: José Baquíjano and the Audiencia of Lima*, 2d ed. (1990). Cloth ISBN 0-8420-2353-4 Paper ISBN 0-8420-2352-6

Carlos B. Gil, ed., *Hope and Frustration: Interviews with Leaders of Mexico's Political Opposition* (1992). Cloth ISBN 0-8420-2395-X Paper ISBN 0-8420-2396-8

Heidi Zogbaum, *B. Traven: A Vision of Mexico* (1992). ISBN 0-8420-2392-5

Jaime E. Rodríguez O., ed., *Patterns of Contention in Mexican History* (1992). ISBN 0-8420-2399-2

Louis A. Pérez, Jr., ed., *Slaves, Sugar, and Colonial Society: Travel Accounts of Cuba, 1801–1899* (1992). Cloth ISBN 0-8420-2354-2 Paper ISBN 0-8420-2415-8

Peter Blanchard, *Slavery and Abolition in Early Republican Peru* (1992). Cloth ISBN 0-8420-2400-X Paper ISBN 0-8420-2429-8

Paul J. Vanderwood, *Disorder and Progress: Bandits, Police, and Mexican Development*, revised and enlarged edition (1992). Cloth ISBN 0-8420-2438-7 Paper ISBN 0-8420-2439-5

Sandra McGee Deutsch and Ronald H. Dolkart, eds., *The Argentine Right: Its History and Intellectual Origins, 1910 to the Present* (1993). Cloth ISBN 0-8420-2418-2 Paper ISBN 0-8420-2419-0

Steve Ellner, *Organized Labor in Venezuela, 1958–1991: Behavior and Concerns in a Democratic Setting* (1993). ISBN 0-8420-2443-3

Paul J. Dosal, *Doing Business with the Dictators: A Political History of United Fruit in Guatemala, 1899–1944* (1993). Cloth ISBN 0-8420-2475-1 Paper ISBN 0-8420-2590-1

Marquis James, *Merchant Adventurer: The Story of W. R. Grace* (1993). ISBN 0-8420-2444-1

John Charles Chasteen and Joseph S. Tulchin, eds., *Problems in Modern Latin American History: A Reader* (1994). Cloth ISBN 0-8420-2327-5 Paper ISBN 0-8420-2328-3

Marguerite Guzmán Bouvard, *Revolutionizing Motherhood: The Mothers of the Plaza de Mayo* (1994). Cloth ISBN 0-8420-2486-7 Paper ISBN 0-8420-2487-5

William H. Beezley, Cheryl English Martin, and William E. French, eds., *Rituals of Rule, Rituals of Resistance: Public Celebrations and Popular Culture in Mexico* (1994).

Cloth ISBN 0-8420-2416-6
Paper ISBN 0-8420-2417-4

Stephen R. Niblo, *War, Diplomacy, and Development: The United States and Mexico, 1938–1954* (1995). ISBN 0-8420-2550-2

G. Harvey Summ, ed., *Brazilian Mosaic: Portraits of a Diverse People and Culture* (1995). Cloth ISBN 0-8420-2491-3   Paper ISBN 0-8420-2492-1

N. Patrick Peritore and Ana Karina Galve-Peritore, eds., *Biotechnology in Latin America: Politics, Impacts, and Risks* (1995). Cloth ISBN 0-8420-2556-1 Paper ISBN 0-8420-2557-X

Silvia Marina Arrom and Servando Ortoll, eds., *Riots in the Cities: Popular Politics and the Urban Poor in Latin America, 1765–1910* (1996). Cloth ISBN 0-8420-2580-4 Paper ISBN 0-8420-2581-2

Roderic Ai Camp, ed., *Polling for Democracy: Public Opinion and Political Liberalization in Mexico* (1996). ISBN 0-8420-2583-9

Brian Loveman and Thomas M. Davies, Jr., eds., *The Politics of Antipolitics: The Military in Latin America*, 3d ed., revised and updated (1996). Cloth ISBN 0-8420-2609-6 Paper ISBN 0-8420-2611-8

Joseph S. Tulchin, Andrés Serbín, and Rafael Hernández, eds., *Cuba and the Caribbean: Regional Issues and Trends in the Post-Cold War Era* (1997). ISBN 0-8420-2652-5

Thomas W. Walker, ed., *Nicaragua without Illusions: Regime Transition and Structural Adjustment in the 1990s* (1997). Cloth ISBN 0-8420-2578-2 Paper ISBN 0-8420-2579-0

Dianne Walta Hart, *Undocumented in L.A.: An Immigrant's Story* (1997). Cloth ISBN 0-8420-2648-7 Paper ISBN 0-8420-2649-5

Jaime E. Rodríguez O. and Kathryn Vincent, eds., *Myths, Misdeeds, and Misunderstandings: The Roots of Conflict in U.S.-Mexican Relations* (1997). ISBN 0-8420-2662-2

Jaime E. Rodríguez O. and Kathryn Vincent, eds., *Common Border, Uncommon Paths: Race, Culture, and National Identity in U.S.-Mexican Relations* (1997). ISBN 0-8420-2673-8

William H. Beezley and Judith Ewell, eds., *The Human Tradition in Modern Latin America* (1997). Cloth ISBN 0-8420-2612-6 Paper ISBN 0-8420-2613-4

Donald F. Stevens, ed., *Based on a True Story: Latin American History at the Movies* (1997). ISBN 0-8420-2582-0

Jaime E. Rodríguez O., ed., *The Origins of Mexican National Politics, 1808–1847* (1997). Paper ISBN 0-8420-2723-8

Che Guevara, *Guerrilla Warfare*, with revised and updated introduction and case studies by Brian Loveman and Thomas M. Davies, Jr., 3d ed. (1997). Cloth ISBN 0-8420-2677-0 Paper ISBN 0-8420-2678-9

Adrian A. Bantjes, *As If Jesus Walked on Earth: Cardenismo, Sonora, and the Mexican Revolution* (1998). ISBN 0-8420-2653-3

Henry A. Dietz and Gil Shidlo, eds., *Urban Elections in Democratic Latin America* (1998). Cloth ISBN 0-8420-2627-4   Paper ISBN 0-8420-2628-2

A. Kim Clark, *The Redemptive Work: Railway and Nation in Ecuador, 1895–1930* (1998). ISBN 0-8420-2674-6

Joseph S. Tulchin, ed., with Allison M. Garland, *Argentina: The Challenges of Modernization* (1998). ISBN 0-8420-2721-1

Louis A. Pérez, Jr., ed., *Impressions of Cuba in the Nineteenth Century: The Travel Diary of Joseph J. Dimock* (1998). Cloth ISBN 0-8420-2657-6 Paper ISBN 0-8420-2658-4

Guy P. C. Thomson, with David G. LaFrance, *Patriotism, Politics, and Popular Liberalism in Nineteenth-Century Mexico: Juan Francisco Lucas and the Puebla Sierra* (1998). ISBN 0-8420-2683-5

June E. Hahner, ed., *Women through Women's Eyes: Latin American Women in Nineteenth-Century Travel Accounts* (1998). Cloth ISBN 0-8420-2633-9 Paper ISBN 0-8420-2634-7

James P. Brennan, ed., *Peronism and Argentina* (1998). ISBN 0-8420-2706-8